GW01454199

All this - and Heaven too?

HELENA EDWARDS

All this -
and Heaven too?

BATH
CRUCIBLE PUBLISHERS

Published by
CRUCIBLE PUBLISHERS
Norton St Philip
Bath BA2 7LA
www.cruciblepublishers.com

First published 2009

ISBN 978-1-902733-07-4

©Helena Edwards 2009
The moral right of Helena Edwards
to be identified as the author of this work
has been asserted in accordance with the
Copyright, Designs & Patents Act 1988

Set in 12/15.5pt Garamond
Printed in Great Britain by
Henry Ling Limited, Dorchester

Acknowledgements

I would like to express my grateful thanks for all their help to Martin Cox, Marilyn Cox, Michael Cox, Ken Duxbury, Ifor Rhys, Robert Twigger and Karole Webster.

HELENA EDWARDS

Contents

1. INTRODUCTION

I was sitting on the front stairs, weeping. I was nine years old. 'Don't go, dad. Don't leave me!'

My father was standing at the front door, his hand upon the latch. His posture was unyielding, his expression cold, distant. His thoughts were in another place - a place I could not reach. He walked out of the door, without a word, closing it gently but firmly. The sound of his footsteps grew fainter.

Then there was silence.

During my childhood, my mother took me to church every Sunday. There were three Services on that day, and we attended all of them. At the age of 12, I refused to attend any more services.

What was the meaning of life, I asked myself, and what was my place in it? I was sure that there was some knowledge which could help me. There was help somewhere, but I did not know how to look for it.

The remainder of my childhood was spent in that house, in the company of my mother and grandmother. My mother was an accomplished pianist. She played by ear and sang in a sweet soprano voice. This was her favourite way of spending an afternoon in the house. My grandfather was a shadowy figure in the background. He had settled for a peaceful life with my grandmother. She was a wonderful woman, who ruled the household. She wore an ankle-length black dress with a black lace stand-up collar, secured with a jet brooch. She had large, capable hands, with bony fingers. She was an expert needlewoman, and made beautiful gowns for my ballroom dancing competitions. She put darts in the waist of my chiffon dress which made the skirt flare out as I moved around the dance floor. I think her skills must have been transmitted in her genes from her mother, my great grandmother, who was head dressmaker in the exclusive salon of Jays, in Regent Street, which outfitted Royalty with their regalia.

The masculine energy, so necessary for the feminine psyche, was sadly lacking in my childhood. But there was pre-science, somewhere deep within me, a conviction that my life was going to change - although I had no idea of the form it would take. This knowledge sustained me throughout my childhood. It was manifested whenever friends or relatives asked me: 'What are you going to do when you grow up?' My answer was usually: 'I want to know the future'.

My mother sent me to a private school in the next street, which featured bible classes every day, with a few lessons in arithmetic, geography, and little else.

My headmistress was the principal reason for my leaving school at the age of 14. She was a short, stocky, middle-aged woman with noticeably short legs and an over-developed bosom, which did not accord with her stature. Her hairstyle was fashionable in the '20s. Her brown hair hung in two plaits over her ears. This gave her a stem expression, especially when her dark eyes glinted coldly with disapproval of a student. She also had an inclination to pout when there was the slightest sign of disobedience.

The fees were high, but my mother insisted upon my attendance there, for she was convinced that, in a larger school, I would be more prone to contact infection. I wanted to attend The Bluecoat School, partly because of the attractive uniform, but also because, in that school, I would have an opportunity to mingle with children in a more expansive environment.

Instead, I attended a school which taught only fifteen pupils. There were no exams. Most of the pupils were apathetic. One of them stands out in my memory.

Dennis Whitty was a fat boy with a big bottom, who wore short, tight trousers. He was always jolly, with bright blue eyes, but never seemed to be interested in anything.

On one occasion, I dared to remark, in front of the class, that I thought the bible readings were over-long. My remark was born of intense boredom with endless descriptions of the circumference of the Ark! I had found that most of the pupils were bored, but never dared to express their opinions about the curriculum.

I noticed that the teacher's neck was beginning to redden, and prepared myself for her disapproval. She strode over to me, and slapped my face.

When I was 14, I contracted measles, and pretended that my condition was serious, in order to prolong my absence from school. Much to my mother's dismay, I refused to return to school.

At the age of 15, I obtained a job at Sainsbury's Head Office in Vauxhall. I worked in a small office writing out slips donatiing charitable sums to worthy institutions.

The bus journeys to Vauxhall were hazardous. The Germans were intent on bombing Battersea Power Station, which was on our route to London.

There were regular frenzied injunctions from the bus conductor: 'Fall to the floor, and lie flat! There are bombs falling all around us!' Well-dressed businessmen, wearing Trilby hats and carrying rolled-up umbrellas, fell beside elderley ladies and smart girls travelling to their offices. We had to reamin in our positions until the bus conductor, who was risking his life at the 'observation post', called out: 'All clear! - return to your seats'.

At the age of 21 I met a man with whom I became infatuated. Unwisely, we got married, and I bore him a son, Martin. The father, Thomas Cox, disappeared a week after the birth, then made several visits to see us. I had decided by this time that I had to start divorce proceedings, since we were incompatible. I had to start working again, to support myself and my son.

But the pattern of desertion in my life, after my father had abandoned me, was destined to repeat, when I met Vasily, a Russian Jew, at Coombe Springs. He was the dearest love of my life. He deserted me for a more exotic lifestyle in the United States, marrying one of the wealthiest women writers in America. She was thirty years his senior, and gradually became deaf and dumb.

He desired wealth, above all else. But he was a creature of opposites: he always displayed, above his door, an image of a skull and crossbones, with the inscription: Memento Mori.

For many of our mutual friends, he was a strong influence for good. He came from a different culture and he was very direct in his approach to life. Vasily was destined to reappear in my life again and again, until his death in Las Vegas in 2002, at the age of 84.

Reflecting upon these earlier periods in my life, I realise that each apparent 'calamity' was succeeded by new vistas which opened up before me, in an extraordinary manner - seemingly by chance.

I was commuting to London every day, whilst my mother was looking after Martin at home. A series of strange coincidences occurred. I was working in an office in a jeweller's store in Hattton Garden. A woman in the office was speaking on the telephone to the American Embassy, about her possible employment in their office.

'If she can do it, then so can I', I reflected. I wasted no time in telephoning the Embassy, and making an appointment. I obtained an excellent position in the Embassy, with

The author, aged about 21

my own office, and a good view of Grosvenor Square.

It was there that I met an American naval N.C.O., George Cornelius, who occasionally came into my office to refer to some correspondence in the files. He was married to the daughter of a bishop.

'Why don't you come to some lectures at a hall in Victoria, to be given by John Godolphin Bennett!' he said. 'The title of the series is: 'What are we Living for?'

A few days later, my new American friend escorted me to the hall in Victoria. I walked into the crowded hall.

Unknown to me, John Bennett was destined to exert a great influence upon my life.

I guessed that he was in his mid-fiftes, and at the height of his powers. He was a handsome, tall man with cornflower-blue eyes, and a magnetic presence; energy vibrated from him.

His wife, Winifred, invited me to visit his community at Coombe Springs, in Surrey, where I began to study his ideas at weekends, and participated in the various inner exercises taught by the Leader, as described later in thjis this book.

Eventually, I decided to live and work in the community, and my son accompanied me. Nine years later, when he was

13 and she was 11, Martin met Marilyn Richardson at a party on the lawn to celebrate the Leader's birthday! In 1961, when he was 19 and Marilyn was 17, they were married. The marriage has lasted over forty years. They had two sons and two daughters. I am now the great grandmother of 10 children.

I became Bennett's secretary, a demanding but interesting job. In this environment, I found that I had certain abilities, which I had never suspected. Bennett had an ability to develop latent capacities in his students. I found that I was able to learn and perform the difficult 39 Movements of Gurdjieff, and was eventually encouraged by the Leader to take classes of students.

It seemed to me that my life in the community was opening up in a way which I could never previously have suspected.

In 1958, after a long period of study of the ideas of Pak Subuh (see Chapter 8) , who had returned to Indonesia, I decided to leave the community, to get a taste of ordinary life. Vasily had been sent to Canada by Pak Subuh, to spread the ideas of Subud throughout the country.

For some months, I lived at Eva Bartok's cottage, nearby, as her companion. She had great ambitions, and wished to become a famous film actress in Hollywood.

I accepted a job in the BBC Light Entertainment Unit at Shepperton, as secretary to the Director of the Unit.

Two years later, I was walking along Coombe Lane, when I heard a voice emanating from a car which had drawn up beside me. The driver was John Bennett.

'Come back!' he said, forcefully.

It was an extraordinary coincidence: At that moment, I had been reflecting upon how meaningless my life had become.

'Yes', I said. 'I will return!'

In a few weeks, I had left my flat in a nearby house, given in my notice to the BBC and moved into the big house at Coombe Springs.

Almost immediately, I met, amongst the people in the community, the man who was destined to become my next husband.

Gilbert Edwards appeared to be in charge of all practical matters in the community. He was highly skilled in many ways, as well as having a degree in Science. From the beginning, my connection with him was not in the intellectual sphere. I was attracted to him because of his eccentricities, and felt the need for a husband. He seemed to appear at the right moment for marriage to take place. So we came together in 1962, and decided to get married.

The marriage lasted for some years. When Coombe Springs was disbanded in 1966, we took a flat on Kingston Hill. For two years I worked in John Bennett's company, Structural Communications.

But inwardly, I was being pulled in another direction. Gilbert came from the North of England, and wanted to settle on the bleak North Yorkshire moors, where a friend had loaned him a large house in a particularly lonely and remote area. I spent sometime with Gilbert under these conditions, and it was apparent that he wished to remain there. But I could not face the prospect of such an existence for any length of time.

One day, I walked out into the back garden, sat down, and reflected upon the situation. I was leaving, and I would never return. I could not spend the rest of my life in this place. Gilbert understood, and accepted my decision, but was unswerving in his desire to stay in this lonely place.

I returned to Kingston, and took a flat near John Bennett's house. At this time, I was drawn towards the idea of spending some months in Morocco. I told John Bennett about my decision. He disapproved, but I had already decided to go ahead. I left my job in Structural Communications, and, in 1969, took a one-way flight to Tangier. My experiences in

Morocco are described in later chapters of this book.

John Bennett had given me an address of a writer in Tangier, Michael Scott, whose house I eventually found in Rue Shakespeare. I knocked on a door in a wall, and his vital face appeared. I was invited in for tea in his exotic tropical garden.

Michael asked me if I would like to meet Professor Ikbal Ali-Shah. He drove me to the house where the Professor lived. I got out, but Michael stayed at the wheel. 'Are you not coming with me?' I asked.

'No, I have something to do in another part of the city' he said!

'But I cannot call at his house unaccompanied,' I said.

'Yes, you can!' said Michael. 'He is a very understanding man, and will put you at your ease!'

I walked round the wide stone steps, on which the Professor's guard was sitting, in Afghan dress. He did not look up, but remained seated, his head bent down.

I walked up the remaining steps to the Professor's front door. There were beautiful, colourful flowering plants on either side.

I rang the bell with some trepidation. An elderly gentleman appeared at the door, wearing a smart Western suit. He peered at me, and asked: 'Who are you'

'Helena Edwards' I said.

'I don't know you! But come in, anyway!'

He asked me to talk about myself. I could always do that! But doing so intentionally was another matter

After that first meeting, I was invited quite often to lunch with the Professor and his housekeeper, Zorah, who was sometimes accompanied by her little daughter Fatima, aged eight. She was a talented dancer, and often gave a charming performance to the sounds of the Professor's gramophone.

Sadly, he died in a motoring accident in the city a few weeks later.

2. COOMBE SPRINGS

A Study of Life and Work in the Community

The Leader was sitting in an enormous, shiny, brilliant red wooden armchair. He spoke in a quiet, disarming voice: 'Why have you come?'

I had attended his course of lectures in London, entitled: 'What are we Living for?', and had been invited to visit his community at Coombe Springs, in order to find out more about his work.

There were about twenty students, sitting cross-legged on the floor in front of him, eagerly awaiting enlightenment.

I was startled by the directness of his manner, and searched frantically in my mind for some kind of answer which would sound plausible - even if untrue. At that moment, it would have taken more courage than I possessed, to answer, truthfully: 'I don't know'. Inviting a possibly hostile reaction from this extraordinary man, was something which I was not prepared to risk.

I was being confronted by John Godolphin Bennett, philosopher and writer, who was said to be transmitting the teaching of George Gurdjieff to a group in London, and at Coombe Springs.

My reply was trite: 'I have come to study the Moving Centre'.

The Leader then gave a discourse, pointing out that man was a being composed of three centres: the Moving Centre, the Emotional Centre and the Intellectual Centre.

I was surprised, and delighted when, later that day, one of Bennett's pupils approached me, and said: 'The Leader has asked me to let you know that you may attend the 'Work

Sundays' regularly. They are held here once a week'.

'Work Sundays' were special days at the community in Surrey. Many students arrived to participate in the working teams. Lunch was prepared in the large kitchen by the cooking team, usually consisting of three women.

During the meal, the Leader introduced various philosophical ideas, based on the teachings of Gurdjieff. During these discourses, students had an opportunity to ask any questions they wished.

Visitors came from many different backgrounds, But we all felt connected by a common aim: to acquire knowledge, and to discover our latent possibilities.

Lists of working teams were prepared during the preceding week, and displayed on the notice board in the main hall. One of the pupils was always selected to act as House Supervisor, whose role was to answer practical questions which might arise during the day.

On my first visit, a kindly man, with the appearance of an academic, approached me, and said: 'We would like you to work with the gardening team. Would you please join them on the lawn.'

I was given a small fork, and a sack upon which to kneel, and instructed to remove the copious weeds from the spacious lawn.

As the team knelt, side by side, we were each handed a list of twelve Tibetan words. 'Please tie these lists around your wrists, and learn the words whilst you are working. You should aim to memorise all of them by lunchtime. One of you may be selected to recite the complete list, from memory, during the meal.'

This was an extraordinary task. It had the effect of replacing my usual fantasies - in which I often indulged when performing simple, undemanding tasks - with intentional mental activity. There was no 'space' in the mind for indulgence in any other mental diversion. The whole of my attention must be divided between the physical work, and the task of learning the words.

I encountered great inner resistance to directing my mental attention in this manner. My mind frequently wandered into daydreams of all kinds.

This was a most important discovery for me. I saw that it was possible to use my mind in intentional mental activity, instead of my mind using my mental energy in whichever way it wished. In my ordinary state, I realized that I had no control over my thoughts. This was a startling discovery, which revealed great possibilities in the mental realm

At lunch that day, the Leader explained the significance of this task:

'The object of this exercise is to switch the attention away from the endless stream of associations, which often take the form of negative thoughts which filter in and out of the mind. We can then conserve mental energy by using our supply of it intentionally, instead of heedlessly dissipating it.

'The stream of associations - the mental dialogue which takes place continuously within our minds - causes a prodigal waste of energy. When this involuntary output is replaced by a volitional use - for example, concentration on Tibetan word lists - we can free part of the supply of energy for transformation into what is termed 'spiritual energy'.

I thought I was beginning to understand these concepts, and felt that they held great possibilities....

THE 'STOP' EXERCISE

I visited the community regularly on Work Sundays, and was often allocated to a gardening team. Occasionally, the Leader strolled round the grounds whilst we were working, and suddenly shouted: 'STOP!'

It had been explained that, when we heard this injunction, we should 'freeze' our postures, thoughts and feelings, and hold that experience, without changing anything, until the command 'CONTINUE' was given.

Students who felt unsteady during the exercise were instructed to fall to the ground, in a relaxed manner. A member of the team felt unsteady, and fell flat upon the path, with his arms outstretched. Others were 'frozen' in odd positions, with forks and spades poised awkwardly in the air.

On one occasion, the postman was walking up the drive, whilst we were in the midst of a 'Stop' exercise. I longed to switch my 'frozen' gaze to observe his reactions - but movement of any kind during the 'Stop Exercise' was strictly forbidden.

I discovered that the position of my body was very different from how I had imagined it to be. I observed that my face and body were often contorted in tension, whist my mind was indulging in some trivial fantasy, which was absorbing my energy. The Exercise revealed the nature of the activity with which my thoughts were occupied for much of the time.

I also caught rare glimpses of the quality of my emotional state.

This 'mirror' of my mental, emotional and physical states, was sometimes far from the imaginary pictures which I had previously enjoyed in relation to myself and my supposed inner activities.

These experiences led me to inner questioning concerning the other moments in time, when I was practising the 'Stop Exercise': what was happening in my inner world, during the greater part of the time, when I was not observing myself? It seemed likely that my image of myself, which I firmly believed to be me, was completely different from the reality!

The Leader made some further comments on this subject. 'This "snapshot" of oneself is a moment of self-observation,' he said. 'It is a technique whereby we can acquire self-knowledge. It operates from a different part of the mind, which is temporarily freed by the "Stop Exercise".'

I realized that my other efforts at self-observation were merely intellectual, and that there was no real 'inner monitor'. The opportunity to observe my associations was valuable. But how could I practise it in ordinary life? It was obvious that it could become merely an intellectual concept, entirely devoid of the dynamic quality of self-knowledge. I suspected that, for some of us, the concept had become, through repetition, a mere idea in the mental realm.

Since writing this book, I have learnt that there are other, more authentic explanations of the purpose of the 'Stop Exercise'.

The Leader introduced other Exercises: the Exercise of Conscious Seeing, and Conscious Hearing, Consciousness of the Sense of Touch, all of which had a profound effect upon my consciousness.

I reflected upon the years of my childhood, and early puberty, when I attended church in London, with my mother. The rituals performed in that church had never enlightened me or given me a sense that there was a possibility for a better quality of life, somewhere within me, not connected with my material existence. The concept of spirituality was still an unexplored realm in my experience.

I was instructed to work on the exercise of Conscious Seeing. It was explained that I should sit, alone, and look at an object, as if I had never seen it before; to keep my attention concentrated upon it, and not to allow my thoughts to be carried away by associations about it, or by any other fantasies.

During this exercise, my imagination often took command, and my attention was drawn away from my focus on

Coombe Springs in the 1960s

photographs on these two pages by Michael Baylis

Volunteers at work on the Djamipoonatra
at Coombe Springs

the central point. But the result, in retrospect, was more akin to what I understood to be a religious experience than all the years of attendance at church

The exercise gave me a strong sensation of my body, and of the present moment. It seemed that I had never, consciously, looked at anything before.

It is relevant here to mention Harry Stubbings. He lived in the community and was an extraordinary man. He occasionally jested, in a kindly manner, about my state of consciousness. He suffered from a progressive muscular disease. His muscles gradually swelled to alarming proportions. However, his sense of humour was brilliant, and we all respected and admired him.

On one occasion I entered his office when he was concentrating on the community accounts. I made an inane remark.

Harry exclaimed, with a humorous note in his voice: 'I do wish that you could expand your present moment!'

His comment enabled me to gain an insight into the idea which he had touched upon, which was important for me to understand at that particular time.

During Sunday lunches, in the huge dining room which looked out upon the lawns and gardens beyond, the Leader introduced certain other exercises.

One Sunday he suggested that we should sit in silence during the meal, and sense the progress of the food as it began the digestive process in our bodies.

I sometimes found it difficult to maintain a proper, serious attitude. I was sitting opposite Katya Petroff, whose face always bore a stern expression. She was equally intent upon her own observations. She had never been known to smile. At times, I saw the humorous side of a situation, and had to restrain myself from bursting into laughter.

The Leader suddenly shouted: 'STOP!' At this injunction,

our knives and forks remained suspended in our hands, and expressions 'froze' upon our faces.

During the exercise, a fly settled upon Katya's nose. Because of the intense atmosphere pervading the room, she commenced to giggle. I was infected by her hysteria, and we both collapsed into helpless laughter.

As a result, the atmosphere became less intense - although I did not feel that this was the intention.

There was a disapproving 'cluck' from the High Table, where the Leader always sat at mealtimes, with his wife, Winifred, and his guests.

Winifred - whom we had nicknamed 'Mrs. B.' - attempted to lighten the atmosphere on these occasions, by making sotto voce remarks to the Leader, when he became a little too severe.

On this occasion, she said, 'Darling - what are we going to have for supper tonight?'

Mrs. B. had an excellent sense of humour - and a sense of humour was essential in such situations.

The waiters, who had been named on the Sunday work-list, had a difficult task. Waiting at table involved carrying individual plates and bowls from the serving hatch in the main hall, into the huge dining room. On some occasions, about 150 people were served at one sitting.

Although the dining room was spacious, the tables were placed end to end, and we were seated close to each other. The waiters manoeuvred around the tables - sometimes during a silent meal. This was unnerving, for there was a rule that plates should be placed on the correct side of the visitors, and taken away from the other side - all to be performed as quietly as possible.

During one of these lunches, a delightful Indian woman asked a waiter, amidst all the chaos, for a finger-bowl. This was, of course, a custom in her country. She later married a younger English undergraduate, whom she had originally met in the community.

A favourite phrase was often repeated by the Leader, in hushed tones, during lunch. This was the injunction: 'We must serve the Work!'

I asked myself: what was 'the Work'?

What did it mean: to 'serve the Work'?

I asked myself these questions many times. Surely this did not consist merely in performing our various tasks, such as gardening, cooking and other duties which were assigned to us?

What was meant by the injunction, and could I carry it out in practice, even if it were explained to me?

Of what did service consist?

Did 'service' take different forms for each of us?

The effort to understand these concepts always left me with a feeling of guilt: I should be doing something, and understanding something - but what was it? I felt like the child in the crowd - except that I was unable to cry out that 'the Emperor had no clothes on'.

I had reached the conclusion that all the pupils, present at these talks, understood the Leader's injunctions. This was a conclusion which I had reached when studying their facial expressions whilst he was speaking: no one questioned him.

Later, I came to understand that this 'blind belief' is one of the outstanding factors in a 'cult' situation - in which no one dares to voice their doubts, since everyone believes in the ideas with which they are being indoctrinated, and will not permit any criticism of the System by other members.

This conclusion has now been verified by many cults. At that time, I did not realize how important it was to question the ideas with which we were being confronted. I tended to accept the teaching as knowledge emanating from Gurdjieff and the Leader. I had no previous experience which would have enabled me to compare and evaluate the ideas which were being propounded.

I realised later that, if I had voiced my bewilderment, this might have been beneficial to me - and to others. I now recall the old adage:

'If one is silent, one is thought to be a fool. But if one opens one's mouth - then it is confirmed!'

My desire for approval far outweighed my desire for truth!

There was a bias towards intellectual activity in the community, which I found disturbing. I felt that my intellectual capacity was not as well developed as some of the more articulate students. But I was not taking into account certain obvious facts about myself. For example, my mechanical habit of judging by appearances. I accepted the ideas as knowledge emanating from Gurdjiieff.

Any remarks suggesting deviation from the 'party line' were certainly discouraged. But they could, on occasions, bring an interesting and valuable reward.

One member, when confronted with an apparently impossible task, remarked: 'This task seems to me to be impossible, because I cannot visualise a non-causal source of initiative!'

The Leader paused for a moment, then changed the subject. But the next morning, the pupil concerned was summoned by Mrs. B., and heartily congratulated. 'Thank God! We have got someone with a mind of his own!', she said.

Hope and fear formed a part of the motivation of our lives. But the voicing of such an analysis was effectively prevented by the assumptions of the members, and the extreme pressure of life upon us. Only the bravest amongst us would dare to criticize the methods. I think that this analysis was made by some of us, many years later.

I recall a certain Seminar which was held at the community. It lasted for three days. When the participants were first assembled in the main hall, a plate of food was handed to each of us, which consisted of an apple, a small loaf of bread, a bottle of water, a meagre portion of cheese, and a few raw vegetables. It was explained that this ration was intended to last for three days.

The programme was then outlined: it consisted of a four-hour reading from Mr. Gurdjieff's book, All and Everything. The reading would be followed by a two-hour 'relaxation' period, during which we had the choice of sleeping, or attending a Gurdjieff Movements class - or simply choosing to relax for that period. This routine was planned to continue, day and night, throughout the three days of the Seminar.

None of us had previously been informed of the programme of events. Prior to this Seminar, I had not understood - or even liked - All and Everything. But the sheer agony of keeping my attention upon the reading for such long periods, eventually led me to an unexpected result: I began to understand parts of the book - and even to think that some of the material was inspired.

As the Seminar progressed, there were minor diversions. One fragile lady - the daughter of a bishop - fainted on the lawn on the first day and was carried off, never to be seen again until the final meeting.

During the long and difficult readings, heads began to nod. On the third day, married couples, sitting together, fell blissfully asleep, heads on each other's shoulders. The food was running out, and so was the energy

When the time came for work on the Gurdjieff Movements, at the 3am 'watch', my stomach felt uncomfortably close to my mouth, and my energy was at its lowest level. Some of the performers in the Movements class were obviously feeling unwell: even the Leader looked ill - but he always put an emphasis on 'beating the body at all costs'. This attitude seemed to be expected of all pupils, and they accepted it as part of life in the community.

It was always emphasized that there was no compulsion to

participate in any of the activities.

Many years later, I understood that it is not the ordinary, everyday part of the human mind - the part which is greedy for possessions, including the possession of knowledge - which is capable of real learning. It is a finer part of the mind which is the bit that is capable of real learning.

The remarkable fact - never mentioned in those days - is that we have to learn how to learn. This is not, as we ordinarily assume, something of which we are all capable, without further tuition.

It became clear that most of us needed to use more commonsense in our daily communal life. Winifred Bennett - an extraordinary woman with clairvoyant powers - often made attempts to restore our sense of humour by her pithy remarks. But a sense of the ridiculous was not encouraged by the Leader. He was endowed with powers of endurance far beyond normal. His aspirations were very high indeed

Occasionally, during a Movements class, he shouted: 'Arms out sideways!' This announcement signified that everyone in the class should raise their arms to the horizontal position, and retain that posture until the Leader lowered his arms.

One day, he told us that he had discovered some sheets of ancient dervish music and, with our co-operation, he planned to give two orchestral performances at the community. I was chosen to play first drum. I had never been at close quarters with a drum, nor had I ever performed in an orchestra.

We were all assembled for action in the Djamichoonatra on the first night. I was seated next to an earnest lady playing double bass in a very professional manner. She later became the third Mrs. Bennett.

This was a new and fascinating experience, for I was surrounded by active musicians - some of whom were professionals. My role was to endeavour to maintain the tempo with a regular beat on the drum.

An entirely new world was opening up before me: I had always been attracted by a challenge.

The difficulty lay in maintaining a strict tempo, as we tended to play our instruments faster and faster. I discovered that I had no more control over my drum than the other musicians exercised over their instruments.

The tempo increased, and the result must have left the audience feeling totally bemused!

The Leader often introduced other experiments - usually as a complete surprise to us. No doubt this was intentional

On another occasion, we were asked to participate in what the Leader termed 'Live Theatre'. We were called upon to play spontaneous roles, gradually involving other characters from the onlookers, in a play, created from moment to moment. Some performers fell naturally into this way of working. But others, who were less relaxed, 'froze' on the stage, and were unable to break through their conditioning into an unfamiliar role.

The Leader also introduced another new idea at Sunday suppers, when the weekend visitors had departed. He provided some wine, and suggested that we should propose toasts to each other.

At one of these events, a charming, auburn-haired lady, Geraldine Rogers, who was sitting at the opposite end of the long table, raised her glass, looked over at me, and called for a toast: 'May she find what she really needs!' she said, forcefully.

That wish, voiced on my behalf, opened up an entirely new way of thinking in my mind. I had never considered my real needs! It seemed to me at that moment that I had always been controlled by my desires! This was a startling proposition: was it possible that my desires might not coincide with my needs?

POSTSCRIPT

It was 1974. I had not seen John Bennett for six years. One evening, three months after his death, I was sitting, reading, at a round table in an old cottage in Kent. Something made me glance up from my book. There, walking towards me, through the 18th century oak door, was John Bennett. His body was as light as air. His face was etched with deep furrows, which afterwards accorded with a photograph which I was shown a few weeks later. It had been taken on the day before his death.

There was a smile of utter, compassionate reassurance upon his face, as he walked slowly towards me. Then the vision disappeared. The experience seemed quite natural to me, and I was unafraid.

3. ROPE-CLIMBING IN THE SWISS ALPS

Some observations on human nature

The community in Surrey was a meeting place for people from many different backgrounds, all seeking a different way of life. I met people there whom I would never have encountered in ordinary life.

Richard Carter was one of John Bennett's students, and visited the community at weekends. We often talked together about our lives, and discovered that our backgrounds were vastly different.

Richard's friend, Victor, who usually accompanied him on visits, mentioned to me that Richard was an expert climber, and often went on expeditions to the Alps.

One day, when we were talking together, Richard remarked: 'I am descended from landed gentry, and my parents live in a stately home in Hampshire. I was born and raised in the family manor. But I am now living in a boarding-house in London, and seeking a new direction for my life.'

I was fascinated by his account of his life as he grew up, with butlers and servants attending to his every need.

It was not long before Richard invited me to his family estate. I was delighted, for I was curious to know more about his aristocratic ancestors, and his stately home.

While we were driving down to Hampshire, my thoughts were turning to the nature of my relationship with this man. I was not physically attracted to him, but was interested in him as a person whose background was completely different from mine.

We reached the gates of the estate, and drove through

acres of woodland, emerging from the forest into a classic scene: a Stately Home, whose pasture land stretched far into the distance.

The manor overlooked an ancient swimming pool, with wide stone steps, which had partly crumbled away. The pool was surrounded by Greek statues of men and women in graceful postures. Richard beckoned to me to enter the house. The interior resembled a scene from another age.

An old butler glided around, giving the impression that he had served there for centuries. With great ceremony, he drew up a chair for me. The room was vast. Paintings of Richard's ancestors peered down from dark corners.

But I sensed that there was something missing from the scene. This room lacked the atmosphere of a home. Now I understood why Richard was seeking a different quality of life.

I was introduced to his elderly parents, who appeared to be on the verge of senility. I realized that Richard had been born of middle-aged parents.

His mother was a genteel, white-haired lady, with a clipped English accent She invited me to her elegantly-laid tea table, where love-birds flitted about, occasionally pecking at the cakes. I was appalled. It seemed so unhygienic! The butler never smiled. His face was always set in a certain expression, as if he had been repeating the same actions for hundreds of years. The other domestics were meek and servile.

Richard's brother, Peter, came in and introduced himself. I sensed at once that he was suspicious of my motives in befriending Richard. He hinted in a veiled manner, voiced in a light, genteel tone, that I might be interested in the family fortune. I was amused at his assumptions, for I had no interest in their financial assets. I was, on the contrary, totally involved in the pursuit of my destiny.

It was a relief when Richard finally bade farewell to his family. I suspected he might have sensed my feelings abut the experience.

When he visited the community again, he said: 'I am going to Switzerland next week, on a climbing expedition in the Alps. Would you like to join me?'

'But I have never climbed a mountain!' I exclaimed.

'You will be quite safe with me. I am an experienced climber,' he said confidently.

'I have no climbing gear' I said.

'Then I will take you to Lillywhite's in London. They will fit you out with a complete climbing outfit.'

My latent sense of adventure was aroused. His generous offer was too enticing to reject. I agreed to accompany him.

His friend, Victor, took me aside. 'I heard from Richard that you will be joining him on his trip to Switzerland. I should warn you that his personality tends to change when he is on a mountain. He becomes reckless, and takes risks, without regard for the difficulties of his companions, who are often less experienced.'

I thanked him for his advice. I knew that the expedition was going to be difficult for me, a novice, to undertake. But I could not resist the opportunity.

We set off by ferry to France, where we took a train to Lausanne. I left my new climbing boots in the Paris Metro, and Richard bought me another pair when we reached Lausanne.

The Alpine train took us to Salvan, a charming little village. It was the point of departure for the expedition. There was only one hotel in the village, and we thankfully sank into comfortable armchairs in the lounge.

Now that the great rocks surrounded us, I had an overwhelming sense that they had a being of their own, and appeared to stretch upwards to infinity. I felt like a tiny, helpless creature beside their massive presence.

But what most disquieted me was Richard's change of

mood. As soon as we arrived in the mountains, he lost interest in my conversation. His expression was one of preoccupation with his own thoughts. I did not know how to deal with this new situation.

'We must rise early in the morning', he said sternly.

The mountain path was near the hotel, and we made for it. We climbed steadily for three hours. Richard was obviously an expert, but, as his friend had warned me, he took risks. He clambered round narrow ledges, with a perilous drop on one side, and expected me to follow him. He never glanced back to see whether I needed assistance.

I was terrified, but followed him as closely as possible. I was becomingly increasingly aware that my very life depended upon him! But he did not appear to care whether I followed him, or not

There was an alternative for me: to be left alone on the mountain-side. But I did not dare to contemplate that. It would mean certain death.

Suddenly, he stopped, and turned round to glance at me. I half expected him to make a complimentary remark about my outfit but, instead, he said, in a grim voice: 'Good climbers climb with their toes turned in!'

I glanced at my feet: they were firmly turned out.

Victor's observation was correct. There was another personality in Richard, previously unknown to me. He had an air of fanaticism, which made me feel distinctly uneasy.

I realized at that moment how little I knew about Richard's inner life, apart from those facets of his personality which had been revealed to me, within a limited set of circumstances.

Reflecting upon the subject of personalities, I was beginning to suspect that there were many different personalities in the human psyche and, for that matter, within myself. These personalities might never be revealed, or even suspected, since they were never evoked by man's ordinary, conditioned existence.

We traversed large areas of scree, a curious phenomenon which consisted of small, loose stones. The climber takes two steps forward, then slides one step back. So progress in those regions is slow.

I slid down long, icy slopes on my buttocks, while the strong rays of the Alpine sun gave me a healthy tan.

Eventually, we arrived at a large mountaineers' hut, where Richard had arranged for us to spend the night. There were many climbers sharing the facilities, who would be setting off on their various routes the following morning, when Richard intended to embark upon the second stage of the climb.

When I thought about what Richard referred to as 'the easy stage', I felt apprehensive, about the second stage, and wondered what awaited us on the heights. I spent an uncomfortable night in the communal hut, fully clothed in my climbing gear, lying on a mattress amongst the other climbers, and awoke to a bitterly cold, grey dawn.

One of the climbers, wearing a thick rope, entwined around his waist, spoke to Richard.

'This is our guide' said Richard. 'I hired him to lead us on the more difficult stage of the climb.'

He had not mentioned the arrangement to me. Now I knew why the guide wore a rope round his waist. I convinced myself that it was only for emergency. My inner conversation consisted of the following reasoning: how could a novice like myself climb on a rope? I dismissed the whole matter from my mind: it was ludicrous!

The guide led us over a hard, steep section of the rock, a climb which took four hours. My only pleasure was the stunning sight of brilliant blue gentians, gradually unfolding their petals on the face of the rock, in the strengthening rays of the sun.

I felt more confident now that the guide was leading us. We arrived at a wide ledge, and he indicated that we should stop for a rest He unpacked some sandwiches, and I made an effort to eat. But I was feeling queasy, for I noticed that the ledge appeared to fall away, a few feet ahead. I could not see what lay beyond. My body was uncomfortably aware that there was an infinite void beyond that craggy edge.

We finished our snack, and lay back to absorb the rarefied atmosphere and stunning panorama surrounding us. But my sensation of fear remained.

The guide suddenly arose, unwound the rope from his waist, and began to tie it around each of our waists, until we three formed a human chain.

He walked swiftly to the edge, stepped over, and disappeared!

I realized that I was next on the rope! I walked slowly to the edge, and unwisely peered over. Mercy! There was a birds-eye view of a village thousands of feet below. A shrieking silence greeted me from the great void. I stared at the huge rock face down which I was expected to descend.

The guide shouted from somewhere far below: 'Madame a peur! Madame a peur!'.

Yes, I was petrified with fear. I knew that I must take the step over the edge. Richard shouted from behind me, in a merciless voice, impatiently waiting to make his descent: 'Go on! If you don't move, no one else can!'

I could not move my legs; they seemed to be paralysed. But then, somehow - and I am sure that my motive was far from altruistic - I put a tense leg over the craggy edge. The sensation of that moment has remained with me as an eternally vivid memory. It was probably the most terrifying moment in my life.

As I stepped over the edge, Richard shouted: 'Turn your body to the rock-face! Don't look down! Stretch your legs, and find the footholds - they are there!'

By what seemed to be a miracle, I found the footholds, and proceeded slowly down the rock face. I glanced up, and saw Richard slowly descending, far above me. I felt the beginnings of something akin to self-confidence. But that feeling was shattered almost immediately. I arrived at a wider gap between the foot-holds. In my state of extreme tension, I could not stretch my leg to reach the next foot-hold.

In despair, I cast my body against the great rock-face. I can still recall the sensation of the sharp, unyielding surface of that rock against my body.

Wild thoughts rushed through my mind at lightning speed: Am I doomed to stay on this rock forever, unable to move up or down? Wasn't there a character in Greek mythology who remained on a rock for all eternity, whilst being devoured by ravens every night?

I felt utterly alone: time seemed to stand still. Despite the horror of my situation, I was very much aware of my body.

Suddenly, the pregnant silence was shattered by the sound of yodelling. A party of Swiss climbers was nearby on the rock face. In my dazed condition, they appeared to be prancing about on the rock, with the ease of young gazelles. They were glancing in my direction, and had obviously understood my predicament.

One of them made his way effortlessly across the rock, and drew level with me. He thrust a bottle, containing colourless liquid, in front of my mouth. 'Buvez! Buvez!' he shouted.

In my state of panic, I would have obeyed any instructions, to enable me to escape from my helpless situation. I took a great swig of the stuff - it was absinthe! My body trembled with the shock. But it had the desired effect I stretched my leg - and found the foothold.

The final part of the descent seemed comparatively simple, and we soon arrived at a large plateau. I lay there, enjoying the aroma of the sweet Alpine grass.

After a few minutes, Richard announced: 'We are going to climb that aiguille over there'.

He pointed to a devilish-looking rock which stretched up to the sky, like a sharp needle. My heart sank. Then, to my infinite relief, he added: 'It is not a suitable climb for a woman'. I thankfully agreed.

But his next statement was calculated to fill me with dread. 'We are going to leave you on this ledge whilst we attempt to climb that aiguille.

We shall have to be quick, because, if you are still on this ledge when the sun reaches its zenith - you will die of sunstroke!'

With my survival in mind, I urged them to hurry on their way, and they trudged through the deep snow, disappearing in the direction of the aiguille.

I remained on the ledge, slowly recovering, and thinking dark thoughts about my companions and their lack of feeling for me. It was then that I heard the sound of heavy footsteps, becoming louder and louder.

But no one appeared. I had visions of the Abominable Snowman. But the sounds gradually grew fainter. It was, of course, another climber making his way across the peaks. I remembered that sounds at this altitude were greatly magnified.

The silence up here was more dynamic than any silence in the world below.

My two companions returned before the sun had reached its peak, and we descended by an alternative route. When we reached the warm valley, we sank down, exhausted, and slept on the sweet-smelling grass for several hours.

Back in my hotel room that night, 1 fell into a troubled sleep. I had nightmares, in which I was crossing precipices, and clambering round dangerously narrow ledges. When I awoke, I sensed that all was not normal with my face. Glancing fearfully in the mirror, I saw that the sun and wind had had a devastating effect upon my skin. My eyes had become mere slits in an unrecognisable, swollen face. My cheeks were bright red, puffed-out balloons.

Then I realized that the only outfit I had brought for leisure evenings, was a shocking-pink cotton dress! This would be a perfect match for my face.

But I was destined to leave the Alps sooner than I had expected. My boyfriend, a young Jewish writer, had become jealous because of my adventures in the Alps with another man. He arrived at the hotel on his motorbike, having driven from England via the ferry.

Archie took me on the back of his motorbike to Paris, where we enjoyed a relaxing weekend, before returning to England.

4. A MEETING WITH A MYSTIC IN PARIS

George Ivanovitch Gurdjieff was born in 1877 in Caucasian Russia. He gathered around him a nucleus of men and women who studied with him throughout Russia and Eastern Europe and, finally, in France, where he lived until his death in 1949.

One of the many features of Gurdjieff's teaching was the concept that our thoughts come to us by association. We are unaware of their origin. They play themselves out, almost disconnected from the rest of our organism. This gives us the illusion that we have a genuine self.

According to Gurdjieff, man has lost himself, because he is unable to act from the real centre of his being.

The first impact of Gurdjieff's teaching was to put in question everything upon which human beings base their lives.

He did not pretend that his teaching was new. He claimed only that it was purer and closer to ancient knowledge than that of his contemporaries. For many of his disciples he existed, not as a person, but as a kind of mirror.

During the early days of the Gurdjieff groups in England, John Bennett made frequent weekend visits to Gurdjieff's apartment in Paris. At this time, the name of Gurdjieff was mentioned in hushed tones in the community.

But one evening in November 1948, the Leader gathered us together in the main hall at Coombe Springs, and announced that we had been selected to visit Gurdjieff on certain weekends, in groups of a dozen pupils. The Leader added that, at the present time, there were countless 'seekers' passing through Gurdjieff's apartment, seeking enlightenment.

I was selected to go to Paris with a group, including

41

some members of Gurdjieff groups in London, whom I had never met.

We set off in several cars, and made the tedious overnight journey by ferry to France, arriving in Paris at midday.

As we were getting out of the cars to enter the Hotel Rena, which was near Gurdjjieff's apartment, someone exclaimed, sotto voce: 'Look!! There's Mr. Gurdjieff'.

He was walking slowly towards us, clad in a full-length, dark blue serge overcoat, with a grey astrakhan collar, and a grey fez. His style of dress gave him the appearance of a tall, commanding figure, although, in reality, he was a short man.

His sudden appearance caused a sensation in our group. Each of us reacted in our own customary manner. One man ran to his car, and busied himself with his luggage. Another dropped his stick nervously, and I ran to pick it up. The rest remained static, silent, awestruck. Someone shouted to me in an authoritative tone: 'Get the luggage out of the boot!'

Mr. G.. (as he was referred to by many pupils) walked slowly and calmly past us, without a sign of recognition. His eyes were focussed above us and far beyond us, as though he was seeking another dimension. He gradually disappeared from sight and merged into the crowded Paris street.

We gathered our luggage and entered the hotel, which was popular with the pupils who visited Mr. G's apartment, as it was known to be the cheapest in Paris.

The Leader quickly assembled us in the lounge, and said: 'You must each choose which "Idiot" you consider yourself to be.'

At the community, he had vaguely referred to Mr. G's 'Science of Idiots' - but we knew very little about it.

He explained that, during the lunches and suppers which took place every day, Mr. G. proposed toasts to his pupils, according to their type of 'Idiot'. He then added certain remarks to the pupil which were intended to offer him (or her), some enlightenment about their psychological or spiritual condition.

There was a geometric series of Idiots, which included 'Round Idiot', 'Square Idiot', 'Zig Zag Idiot', and other types of 'Idiot' in this series. At times during the toasts, he also referred to 'Compassionate Idiot', 'Hopeless Idiot', and other forms of 'Idiot'.

We were confronted with what seemed to be an impossible choice. We knew less about ourselves than we had assumed, and we knew even less about the 'Science of Idiots'!

I chose 'Round Idiot' - by intuition, it seemed - and this was later confirmed by Mr. G. during a toast directed to me.

During my visits to the apartment, I became desperately aware that my life was being formed by a repetitive cycle of events. I felt instinctively that the same patterns of experience would recur again and again in my life. I could not envisage any form of escape from this dilemma. This inner confrontation seemed to have no connection with my experience here, in this apartment. It was merely a sudden realization of the course which my life was most likely to take. Faced with this situation, I was becoming ever more desperate. A recent, unsuitable marriage, ending in divorce, had deepened these feelings of helplessness. Hence my choice of 'Round Idiot' - idiot all the time, I reflected.

By a strange coincidence, I had recently read P.D. Ouspensky's The Strange Life of Ivan Osokin - the philosopher's only novel. The theme of this book is the life of the hero, Serge, who is repeatedly faced with events in his life which end in disaster.

A few years later, I was selected by the Leader to play the role of Zinaida, the unfortunate heroine of the novel. Bennett presented the play at Coombe Springs.

The lunches held by Mr. G. commenced at 1pm with a reading, followed by the meal. This pattern was repeated in the evening, commencing at 8pm, followed by supper. It ended at about 2am.

Later that evening, the Leader took us to Mr. G's apartment. That experience is indelibly imprinted upon my consciousness.

I walked into a narrow, dark hallway. The walls were covered with paintings of every description. Later, I heard that some were valuable, others worthless.

Mr. G. never permitted daylight to enter the apartment. The blinds were always drawn, and the electric lights fully on.

The aroma in that place was unforgettable: the use of strong Eastern cooking spices had blended into an exotic perfume which permeated every corner of the apartment.

I was ushered into a small room leading out of the passage. We sat on cushions on the floor. A reading was in progress, from Mr. G's book, All and Everything. It was the chapter entitled 'Heptaparaparshinokh' (The Law of Seven). This chapter was particularly difficult to comprehend - and it was being read in French.

The journey had been arduous, which may have accounted for my lack of attention. But the irony of the situation was that I had been eagerly awaiting this opportunity, for some weeks.

As I was sitting there, with my head down, immersed in my thoughts, I suddenly felt an impulse to look up. I saw an old man facing me, sitting in a dark corner of the room. He was wearing a red fez and carpet slippers. It was Mr. Gurdjieff! What struck me most forcibly was his ability to render himself almost invisible. He appeared to be as ordinary as everyone else in the room. He appeared to be an old man, sitting in a corner. He looked weary and unwell; but yet, there was something about his presence. I sensed that he was not of this domain.

It occurred to me that this occasion must have given Mr.

G. an opportunity to observe our behaviour. Some visitors had nodded off to sleep; others, like myself, had managed to remain awake, but had encountered the utmost difficulty in summoning sufficient attention to listen, even if they could not understand the meaning behind the words.

Later, we were led into the small dining room, which seated about forty guests. Many of them were strangers to me. Everyone found a place at table, despite the presence of a ritual. Some people -who appeared to be familiar with the routine - formed a chain into the kitchen. Perhaps this was considered to be a more efficient method of serving - but the food was never really hot when it arrived

The soup was rich, with lumps of meat and fat floating on the surface. A choice of drinks was offered: a powerful alcohol known as Marc, or dark red, fiery vodka.

The toasts had already begun. The women were asked to drink a third of their glass for each toast. The men were expected to drink a full glass of alcohol each time a toast was proposed.

I recognized the toastmaster, sitting beside Mr. G. He was Reginald Hoare, whom I had seen at meetings at Colet Gardens, the headquarters of the Gurdjieff activities in London. Before each toast, Mr. G. appeared to give whispered instructions to him. I presumed that Mr. G. was referring to each person's particular 'Idiot'.

The toastmaster then proposed the first toast, uttered in his deep, penetrating voice: 'Here's to the health of all Square Idiots - and to your health, Mr. Jones, who are also one!'

Mr. G. then added certain remarks, sometimes spoken in a strange language. But when he intended a comment for a particular person, it was voiced, for example, in English, so that there could be no mistaking his meaning. One of the pupils described to me an incident concerning a woman who used to attend the ritual meals. She was highly religious, and figured prominently in work for the Church. One evening, when she was present at supper, Mr. G. made some scathing remarks about religion. She got up, and shouted at him: 'I will never come here again!'

She walked out of the apartment, and was never seen there again.

I noticed a remarkable woman, who always sat opposite Mr. G.. She had shining white hair which framed her Madonna-like face, and stunning dark eyes. I heard later that she had worked with Mr. G. at the Prieure in Fontainebleau in the '20s, where he created a centre for his work.

During one of the meals, she turned her head and looked at me with a dazzling smile. It was a glance of great purity and power, which seemed to breathe the quality of love towards me. That moment was timeless, and I can instantly recall it, with all its richness, as if it were in the present moment. In the midst of my bewilderment, the experience seemed to come from another dimension.

During the meals Mr. G. often played a hand organ which resembled a small concertina.

Some people were profoundly moved by the sounds. I found a deep sadness in the music - yet it seemed to lack emotional content. Lise Tracol, an outstanding, dark-haired young woman of considerable presence, attended to Mr. G's needs at table. She procured tape-recordings when he needed them. She was also responsible for some of the cooking. I had seen her performing in the 39 Movements of Mr. Gurdjieff, in London, at Colet Gardens, and had greatly admired her precision and posture. She later married Alfred, who was a superb teacher of the 39 Movements. Tragically, he died of cancer a few years later.

During the meals, Mr. G. offered certain items of food to the pupils Some of them decided that they should eat these delicacies, even though they did not always like them. Others rejected the morsels. This was an interesting dilemma. Some accepted the food, thinking that Mr. G. wished them to do so. Others used their common sense in the choice.

There was no doubt that in these situations, Mr. G.. was able to observe people's behaviour, and come to some conclusions.

I became acquainted with a wealthy woman, whom some pupils at the apartment referred to as 'the richest woman in the Work'. She was known as Melissa Marston (later Mrs. Marston-McCloud). She used to visit the community in England, and was one of Mr. Bennett's friends. She was the daughter of Sir Charles Marston, the historian. Melissa made several visits to Paris to see Mr. G. When she was talking with him one day, he said: 'Come to the supper tonight. I have something to say to you.'

Melissa did not appear that evening. But the following morning, she came to the apartment, and apologized to Mr. G. 'I'm sorry, I was unable to attend the supper last night.'

'*Your* loss!' he retorted.

When she recounted this incident to me, there was a very sad note in her voice.

During this time in Paris, I became uncomfortably aware that all the structures which gave me comfortable support in England were being stripped away. I felt that I was in a totally alien environment, and did not understand anything that was being said or done. I could not rely upon any of the 'crutches' which had supported me in ordinary life. I had a curious sensation of being suspended in a strange world, which was not of my own choice. I did not even know why I was here!

The combination of rich food and strong alcohol was causing me to feel nauseated, and I looked around for a way of escape from the room, without being noticed. I made my way, as inconspicuously as possible, to the door. As I passed Pierre Elliot, he handed me a huge white handkerchief. I fled down the stairs and into the street. As soon as I breathed fresh air, I recovered, returned upstairs to the dining room, and slipped into my seat at Mr. G's table. No one appeared to notice the incident. But, later, Pierre told me that, during my absence, Mr. G. had called out: 'Don't worry about her! She is Blonde No. 24! She will come back!'

After that incident, I was impressed with the reactions of the English toastmaster. When my glass was empty, he filled it with a small quantity of alcohol,; it was just sufficient for me to participate in the toasts. I was astonished at Reginald Hoare's ability to consider my needs, in the midst of the many demands being made upon him by Mr. G.

Later that evening, the toastmaster announced: 'Here's to the health of all Round Idiots, and to your health, Joan Cox, who are also one!'

Mr. G. then added, in his inimitable English accent: 'Joan everybody ! Joan Germany! Joan France! Joan everywhere!'

I should explain to the reader that this was my name until my second marriage. Later, my Christian name was changed to 'Helena' at the suggestion of an Indonesian mystic, Pak Subuh (see chapter seven, 'The Coming of Pak Subuh').

It is significant that I had never felt in harmony with my official Christian name, and preferred the name 'Helena', with its pleasant vowel sounds

The words which Mr. G. had uttered held no significance for me at that moment. At certain times in my life, I have had a flash of intuition, and caught a glimpse of their meaning in relation to my life. But that flash of understanding has always been elusive. It vanishes again , in an instant. But the experience at the time the words were uttered, was electrifying. I felt what seemed to be a metaphysical blow upon the centre of my forehead. That sensation remained with me until I left the apartment at 2am.

As I left, I began to weep. It was a strange, impersonal weeping, and uncontrollable.

An old friend, Rowland Kenny, who was the editor of a leading newspaper, and a pupil of Mr. G., accompanied me as I walked through the streets of Paris, sobbing bitterly. My English habit of caring what strangers thought of me had vanished. Was it possible that Mr. G. had been referring to this habit? Was that what his words were intended to convey? This negative characteristic was a state in which the ordinary, mechanical mind was in control and there is no inner judgement of a situation. This state is referred to in the Work as 'Inner considering'. No inner judgment of a situation.

Upon reaching my hotel, the weeping ceased, as suddenly as it had begun. I went peacefully to sleep.

At lunch the next day, I was relegated to what was referred to as 'The Calves Table' which was situated behind the main table. Most of the young women were seated at that table, There, it was possible to see and hear everything that ensued. Mr. G. often used the phrase: 'The danger of dying like dirty dog if we did not work consciously upon ourselves in life.'

But the meaning of this injunction was obscure.

Before I returned to England, I put certain questions to myself How could I consciously work upon myself in life? How could I acquire self-knowledge?

How could I use my time in a more constructive manner? Where could I find answers to these questions?

Mr. Gurdjieff died in 1949. His last words were as follows: 'Je vous ai laissé dans une merde jolie!' (I have left you in a pretty mess!)

5. THE 39 MOVEMENTS OF MR. GURDJIIEFF

From the Monasteries of Central Asia

Dance patterns derived from an antediluvian tradition in the East, became an integral part of the activities in the community.

One evening at dinner, I heard strange chords on the piano in the next room, which also served as an exercise room. The music was in the minor key, and had an Eastern flavour. The sounds had a strong effect upon my feeling state, which I did not understand. This was a new experience. There was something almost sacred in the chords.

Mrs. B had noticed my interest, and leant forward to suggest that I should take part in the activities in the adjoining room.

I stood at the end of the long room, watching the Movements. The pupils were attempting to coordinate a series of postures, consisting of arms, legs and head movements. The three series were being taught separately. Then the class was instructed to swiftly combine the three series and perform the complete movement, entitled: The First Obligatory.

The tutor, Pierre Eliot, suddenly shouted to one of the performers: 'Stop picking your nose!'

I was shocked, for, under these circumstances, the remark appeared to be distasteful. But, later, when I began to understand something about the purpose of the Movements, I realized that the teacher had been drawing attention to the fact that the pupil was unconscious of most of his bodily movements, and generally moved his limbs without awareness, thus wasting valuable energy.

When, some weeks later, I first met Mr. Gurdjieff in Paris, I noticed that one of his most remarkable features was his economy of movement. His movements appeared to come from an inner, very relaxed, monitor.

One of the purposes of the Movements was to acquire sensation, that is, awareness of the body. I seemed to have a natural aptitude for the Movements, and began to learn the six Obligatory Movements. These had to be learned before attempting the more difficult series of the 39 Movements. They were accompanied by the extraordinary music which Mr. Gurdjieff had brought from monasteries in Central Asia.

The work in the classes was intense, and the discipline severe. We had to work in unison, and in exact time with the music. We had to work in harmony, and in exact time with the row in front of us, moving as they moved.

I performed behind a French woman, who had worked on the Movements in Paris with Mr. G. She was unpredictable. I was told to follow her every movement, with precision.

We worked consciously, by the practice of inner sensation, to refine our postures as near as possible to the perfect position, whilst paying close attention to the timing of the music - which was very difficult for Western ears. We also had to to work for precision.

Whilst performing these Movements, it was impossible to indulge in idle thoughts - or, indeed, to indulge in any thoughts at all. Our whole attention was needed, for the music and for the Movement.

Most of the performers had their own bodily quirks, such as bent wrists, crooked arms, or some other problem. But one of the objectives was to overcome our defects in the quest for the ideal posture, which must be found by the practice of sensation.

My tendency was to perform the Movements in my own habitual way. One of the aims was to violate habitual postural patterns, whilst conforming to group patterns.

The Movements also revealed traits in personality. Someone who tended to be 'pushy' in life, was often out of line, and ahead of the others. This was not permitted in the class.

During this period of intensive study, I noticed that my perceptions were heightened. I became more aware of my surroundings, and had a strong sensation of my body. It seemed as though I was watching it from somewhere outside myself.

The Movements which we were being taught became increasingly difficult. Sometimes, I was told to repeat a series of Tibetan words, whilst performing a complicated 'canon', in which each row took on a different role and performed a different series of Movements.

It was said that the Movements had a beneficial effect upon every organ of the body. Each movement was designed to improve the functioning of a particular organ.

Mention should be made here of the heroic efforts of the pianists accompanying these classes. Leon Flamholc and John Perrott, amongst many other musicians, had a very difficult task. The tempo and timing had to be carefully maintained, amidst frequent stops by the instructor, in order to explain certain points to the students.

Some members found the Movements impossibly difficult to learn. Many assumed that they were already aware of their bodies. But when their minds had to give an order to their bodies, they found that there was little connection between the two. The result sometimes set up an inner conflict. This caused some pupils to give up in disgust, and walk out angrily whilst a class was in progress - vowing never to return.

But those who persevered, often made a breakthrough, and struggled with difficulties in their bodily mechanism.

A student who had studied the Movements for many

years, remarked to me recently that he had never lost the consciousness of his body which he had acquired whilst working on the Movements.

After I had made a long and arduous study of the 39 Movements, the Leader asked me to start a Movements class. This was a difficult undertaking, because I had to teach very complicated Movements. I also had to handle the psychological aspect of the classes, in which the students were finding certain Movements almost impossible to master.

The Leader also instructed me to devise a new Movement every week, and to teach it to the Sunday class. This was one of the most difficult tasks with which I had ever been confronted. But, somehow, I managed to produce what was required, in a geometrical form. This was a great challenge, and I often felt poised between necessity and impossibility, in spite of the efforts of the accompanying pianists, particularly Leon Flamholc and John Perrott. The tempo and timing of the music were all-important, and they had to be prepared for frequent stops by the teacher. We were called upon to perform in the Djamichoonatra, the nine-sided building which had been designed by Frank Lloyd Wright, and constructed by certain students who were professional builders. The audience consisted of some of the Leader's friends, and members of the public. The Leader had announced that this building should be reserved for 'higher activities'.

When performing the Movements, the students wore a garb consisting of white baggy trousers, and long white shapeless smocks, all made from parachute silk. Each row wore sashes of a different colour. The ensemble was completed with gold bands worn around the head.

I found these public performances difficult, and was always repelled by the necessity to perform before a large public audience. One day, the Leader, who was aware of my feelings in the matter, handed me a close-up photograph of

Mr. Gurdjieff, instructing me to sit alone, and direct my attention to the photograph for a few minutes every day.

The exercise had the effect of calming my feelings, and clearing my mind before the performances.

The Leader alleged that esoteric meanings were attached to each Movement.

When we had learned the positions, we began to work on perfecting our postures. This was done by what was referred to by the Leader, as a sort of 'policeman in our inner being', who watched our Movements so that we executed them as perfectly as possible.

At this time, I, together with other English students of the Movements, joined the French group in Paris, to make a private film of the Movements, in a professional film studio in St. Denis.

We were sitting in front of the leader of the French group, a beautiful, dominating woman named Madame Jeanne de Salzmann. She looked around the room, and remarked forcefully: 'Someone will be needed to look after the costumes.'

Oh, I thought, that cannot be me, because I am needed for the movements group.

But her eagle eyes focussed upon me. 'You,' she said in a piercing tone, 'will be the wardrobe mistress!'

This was not what I had expected, for I had thought that I would be placed in a prominent position in the class. Such is the ego! But, eventually, I was given a place in the class.

On one occasion, when we were performing the Movements in London, at Colet Gardens, Thomas de Hartmann played the accompaniment for No. 2 of the 39 Movements. He must have touched the chords so lightly that I could hardly believe that they were being played by human hands. It was as though, in some mysterious way, the piano was playing itself, and that the sounds were reaching me through the ether.

Listening to the recital, played in that way, was an extraordinary experience. This remains within me. I hardly recognized the music, which I had often heard, as we performed the Movement.

I never met Mr. De Hartmann, but on one occasion, I passed him on the stairs at Colet Gardens. At that moment, I felt that I knew him in a different way, more directly, and that he belonged to another domain

At times, I asked myself: What was the purpose of all this activity? Could this be progress on the path of human spirituality?

6. THE WOMAN ON THE BUS

I was standing in a crowded old bus in Istanbul, clinging to a shiny leather strap to steady myself, whilst the driver careered around corners at breakneck speed.

My attention was drawn to a woman sitting near me. She looked old and weary; her skin had an unhealthy pallor. Deep lines were etched in her face, and her hair hung in thin grey wisps over her ears. She seemed lonely, and I was sure that she had endured great suffering at some stage in her life. Yet, despite her appearance, I sensed a quality about her which was not ordinary.

I noticed that she was scribbling on a scrap of paper. Then she stood up, and thrust a note into my hand, on which was written: 'Ring me tonight, and I will give you lunch tomorrow. Zona Kardar'. She had added a telephone number.

Then she got off and disappeared amongst the motley crowds ceaselessly passing to and fro in this vast city. I was curious, and wanted to find out more about Zona's life. I was alone in Istanbul, and felt a need for human contact. I rang Zona that evening, and she gave me precise directions to her house.

It was 1951. I had travelled to Turkey from the community in England where I lived, worked and studied the ideas of Gurdjieff and Ouspensky. The Leader had sent me on this journey to deliver a sealed envelope to a Chelebi, the Head of a Mevlevi Whirling Dervish Order, who lived in Istanbul.

The leader had encouraged me to gain experience of travelling alone in foreign countries. I welcomed his suggestion, for it was a great contrast to the sheltered life which I had lived in my childhood.

The next morning I hailed a dolmus - an Istanbul taxi - which was eventually shared with six other passengers who had boarded at various points, as is the custom here.

Zona's house was not negotiable by taxi, and the driver dropped me off at the nearest point.

The road, which inclined steeply downwards, consisted of large, irregular cobblestones, protruding from the ground, which made the descent hazardous. My thoughts turned to Zona. I wondered how she had survived in such a hostile environment. This was, indeed, ancient Istanbul.

I fixed my eyes firmly upon the uneven, dangerous ground, but occasionally glanced up to look at the passers-by. Their unfriendly expressions conveyed their attitude towards me: I had no right to be here. My Western conditioning was slipping away, and I felt increasingly uneasy. This part of Istanbul was far from the tourist beat

I suddenly noticed a little corner shop, and dived into it, seeking reassurance, and a gift for Zona. The shop was gloomy, and had a musty atmosphere. I sensed that the products had remained on the shelves for some considerable time.

But the woman behind the counter was delighted to see me, and greeted me with true Turkish hospitality. Her warm dark eyes glowed with friendship. She wore a long, dark red silken dress, and was pleasantly plump.

I chose a box of Turkish Delight from the shelf. She seemed to think that it was a great joke that I was shopping in her little store.

Tesdakur ederim' (thank you) I said, as I was leaving the shop.

The Leader had conducted a crash course in Turkish before I left for this trip. He was a Turkophile, having lived in Istanbul for many years. As I left the shop, I realized that my contact with a friendly human being had restored my positive attitude to life.

I turned into the Street in which Zona lived. It was narrow, and lined with shabby houses on either side. Glancing up, I saw women in traditional garb scowling down at me from their windows. A Western interloper had dared to invade their territory! Young girls, clad in brightly-coloured silken pantaloons, darted in and out of front doors, casting resentful glances at me. I felt like an unwelcome stranger, as I hastily made my way along the ancient Street.

Large piles of wood and coal were stacked in the gutters, ready for the brief but bitterly cold winter, when the long path of cobblestones was covered by a sheet of ice, and shopping was confined to the little store which I had visited.

Eventually, I heard a voice from the terrace above: 'Helena! Here I am!' Zona's grinding, husky voice was penetrating, but kindly.

I climbed the ancient, barren stone steps, stained by Time, and felt a great sense of relief as Zona ushered me in.

Her sitting-room was exotic. It had that mystical quality which old Turkish houses often acquire. Her apartment was pervaded with an indescribable atmosphere. I thought that she had sustained many rich experiences in that house.

I was reminded of a visit I had made to Pierre Loti's house on the banks of the Golden Horn. He was the French writer who had helped to release the Sultan's slave girls, by writing to them in French, a language which most of them understood. In his letters, he revealed the terrible restrictions on their lives in the harems, and showed them that it was possible to live a free life. It was the beginning of emancipation for them.

Such ancient Turkish houses have an atmosphere of relaxation which is unknown in the West.

'I live on £40 a month' said Zona. 'I speak eight languages, and teach the artisans working in this vicinity.'

Richly-coloured carpets adorned her floors, and the walls

were covered with beautiful paintings, and esoteric designs.

'How did you acquire these exquisite treasures?' I asked. I was overwhelmed by the beauty of her surroundings.

'Payment from my pupils!' she said, with a beaming smile.

'I am a German Jewess, and have lived here, amongst Moslems, for forty years. It has not been easy.'

She continued: 'All my relatives were murdered in Auschwitz. I was released from the camp by the Nazis, who discovered my talent for languages, and sent me to work in Istanbul. At that time, Turkey needed cultured people who were linguists' Zona was 84, and laughingly referred to herself as 'an infidel'. She was diabetic, and had recently undergone surgery for cancer.

Whilst she was preparing lunch, I sat on silken cushions in her sitting-room, feasting my eyes upon the colours of her furnishings,.

Glancing out of the window, I glimpsed a bizarre scene, far below.

A gypsy woman, clad in a full, brightly-coloured skirt, was carrying a basket of herbs, which she was selling to passers-by. A man nearby - who was possibly her husband - was beating a bear, to make it dance, in order to earn money. The poor, unhappy aninimal was chained, and foaming at the mouth.

I heard Zona calling: 'Helena! Lunch is ready!'

She served an unusual, delicious meal, skilfully blending a combination of Turkish and Jewish ingredients. She had prepared Turkish soup, made with chicken and barley. This was followed by a succulent Jewish stew, made with beer, potatoes and spices, which was known as cholent. Dessert consisted of the traditional baklava, oozing with exotic honey

At the end of the meal, I turned to thank Zona for her hospitality.

'I may not have much longer to live, and friends mean so much to me!' she said.

Travelling back to my hotel later that evening, I reflected upon my meeting with Zona. It seemed that we had something in common - a kind of loneliness. I was becoming increasingly interested in meeting people from other cultures , and participating in their way of life.

My thoughts turned to the mission which I had undertaken. Tomorrow, I must find the Chelebi's house, situated somewhere in this great city.

7. ACROSS THE ANATOLIAN PLATEAU

In Search of a Chelebi

I awoke early the next morning, and began my search for the Chelebi's house, which was in the Omar Khayyam Caddesi. I had no map, and relied upon directions from passers-by. But none of them had ever heard of the street which I sought. Finally, a man, who spoke English, gave me precise directions.

I was again fortunate: there, partly obscured by overhanging leaves, was the magical sign: Omar Khayyam Caddesi. In a few minutes, I had located the Chelebi's house: It was a charming old wooden building, standing alone in a picturesque background of trees and woodland.

I rang the door-bell, and waited.

The door opened a few inches, and a diminutive, hook-nosed old woman peered out suspiciously from the dark recesses of the hall. Her scraggy body was covered with a full-length black cotton dress. I thought she might be a centenarian.

She opened the door a few more inches.

'Can I see the Chelebi, please?' I asked.

'No' was the curt reply. 'He lives in Arsuz, with his family, during the summer months.'

I was surprised at her knowledge of English.

Thoughts flashed through my mind: I was here for another week. Gurdjieff, the Russian philosopher, had once said to me: 'When you are on a spree, go the whole hog - including the postage!'

It was at that moment that I realized how important it was for me to have an objective in my life - it energized me, and would enable me to carry out my mission.

I made a SNAP decision. 'Please may I have the address of the Chelebi in Arsuz', I asked.

I was amazed at my own audacity. The Chelebi was an important man - the Head of a Whirling Dervish Order - and I was a stranger to this old woman. But I was discovering a new confidence in myself, and an ability to meet a challenge, when faced with the need to make a decision.

The housekeeper seemed to trust me, for she disappeared into the dark hall, and soon emerged with a piece of paper which bore the address of the Chelebi. It was written in a spidery hand, which seemed to relate to her emaciated form.

She gave me a map, which revealed that Arsuz was a small town in the south-east of Turkey, on the Mediterranean route to Syria.

I decided to make the journey through Central Turkey, some hundreds of miles across the Anatolian Plateau, and through the Taurus Mountains. It was August, and I knew that the heat in Central Turkey would be unbearable. But my newly found appetite for adventurous travel was stimulated by the thought that I could achieve my mission whilst, at the same time, taking the opportunity to meet the Chelebi, which was a challenge I could not ignore.

I discovered that a bus travelled across the Anatolian Plateau to Iskanderun, the ancient city named after its most famous son, Alexander the Great. There, I could board a local bus to Adana - which was still some forty kilometres from Arsuz. But now, I felt confident that I would find some way of getting to my destination.

The Plateau was arid and dusty, and the heat was intense. The driver stopped every half-hour to refresh us with liberal quantities of fragrant lemon eau de cologne, which he poured into our cupped palms.

Small bands of horsemen, wearing baggy trousers and richly-embroidered leather jackets, galloped across the vast plains surrounding us. I caught glimpses of their faces: their eyes were narrow and slanted, with fierce expressions. I was told that they came from the Steppes of Central Asia.

Small groups of carpet-weavers sat cross-legged, working out their rich, intricate designs on huge carpets spread out on the Plateau. The driver warned us not to get off the bus, as it was dangerous to walk amongst these tribal people.

As we drove across the Plateau, I reflected upon a discourse given by the Leader of the community, before I left for Turkey. The subject of his talk was 'Man's Possibilities'. He had adjured us to discover and develop our latent capacities. He said that most people lived and worked far below their potential. I felt that I was beginning to understand what he meant. This journey was certainly revealing qualities in me which I had never before suspected

I had been feeling unwell, and realized that I had contracted the usual 'bug', from which Westerners often suffer in hot countries. Eventually, it became imperative for me to get off. Somehow, I managed to communicate my predicament to the driver: he stopped, and pointed to an extraordinary contraption out on the plain, surrounded by a ring of mud! There was a flimsy cover above it, and a few boards surrounded it. In desperation, I made a dash for it, not caring that the bus was full of passengers - mostly men!

We were now entering the Taurus Mountains, and the driver pointed to the hieroglyphs, carved out of the rock by Alexander and his army, as they passed by. The driver was following the route which they had taken, many centuries before....

Soon, the driver announced proudly: 'Iskanderun!'

We had reached the historic city in which Alexander was born, to become a conqueror of many lands. I longed to explore the ancient part of the city, to look for possible traces of his life. But the bus was waiting to take passengers to Adana, and only a few more days remained to me before I must return to Istanbul, to take the train to London. I reluctantly boarded the bus for the short journey to Adana.

There, my limited store of Turkish was ineffective; suddenly, I understood why: the men standing around the bus were speaking in Arabic.

This part of Turkey appeared to be male-dominated. There were no women in the streets, and the men were dark-skinned, and mostly bearded. I felt increasingly uneasy, as I tried to assess the situation.

Small groups stood, surveying me, with hostile expressions: a young Western woman, travelling alone, in this remote part of their country, was a startling phenomenon. I suddenly felt vulnerable, and in desperation asked one of the men standing nearby:

'Bus to Arsuz?'

The word 'bus' has a multi-lingual meaning. He understood, and uttered a brusque, unfamiliar sound, which, by his expression, I took to mean 'no'.

I felt increasingly intimidated by their expressions. Thoughts raced through my mind: this situation could become ugly. I was an intruder!

At that moment, a pleasant, fair-haired young man stepped forward, and said boldly: 'I take you to Arsuz on my motorbike!'

His intervention at that moment had changed the situation. I looked closely at him. He was about twenty years old, I guessed, and had an open expression. I felt that I could trust him.

'Evet! (Yes) - I will go with you!'

Now, there was an unfamiliar note in my voice - a note of fearlessness. I clambered on to the back of his motorbike, and we set off along the shores of the Mediterranean. As we passed through charming little villages, people waved to us and greeted us in Turkish.

I was congratulating myself on having found a man who was both helpful and polite.

But, suddenly, without warning, he braked, stopped the bike, looked back at me, and slapped his hand upon my knee.

'Hayir!!' (No), I shouted.

Perhaps it was the sound of his own language, spoken by a Westerner, which startled him. He immediately withdrew his hand, and started up the bike. We were again on our way.

When we reached Arsuz, I offered him some cash for the journey. But he graciously refused it, and we parted with friendly farewells.

Arsuz was a small, friendly town, and everyone seemed delighted to see a Western woman in their midst.

I stopped a kindly looking, elderly man to ask for directions to the Chelebi's house. I knew now that my fear of approaching strangers was a result of my conditioning in childhood.

'Never speak to strangers!' was a maxim often repeated by my family.

But I was learning that I needed to have contact with other human beings - and that I gained energy - and nutrition - from the interaction.

The stranger, who introduced himself as Omar, invited me for an iced drink at a nearby café, and we sat outside, basking in the sunshine, while Omar recounted his tales.

'There is an ancient city buried beneath the sea in this bay', he said, 'but the authorities cannot afford to excavate it.'

Like most Turks, Omar was proud of his little town, and friendly towards Westerners.

The storyteller continued his tales, recounting a legend about Alexander the Great.

'When Alexander was conquering Turkey' he said, 'he advanced with his army towards the forces of Darius, instructing his soldiers to position their shields in such a manner that they reflected the brilliant sunlight on to the enemy forces, thereby blinding them, and winning the battle against Darius.'

Omar was a master storyteller. Like all good storytellers he had the gift of being able to transport the listener to the actual scene of the story.

Omar guided me to the house of the Chelebi. It was situated in glorious surroundings, and I could hear the sound of the waves as they lapped softly on the shore behind the house.

I knocked on the brass-studded door and a tall, stately figure emerged: it was the Chelebi. He was a powerful man, with dark, penetrating eyes, set wide apart, and an aquiline nose. I guessed his age to be about 45. I noticed that he was wearing Western-style clothing: his slim, elegant figure was clad in a well-cut light grey suit.

He was less like a guru than anyone I had ever met!

He greeted me warmly, and ushered me in.

I had called upon him without an appointment - something which I would never have done in England with such an important man. But he was most cordial.

'Please come in, and spend the day with us!' he said, in a warm, cultured voice. He spoke perfect English.

It was a pleasure to meet his wife and two daughters, who greeted me as though I was a long-lost relative!

'Later, you must come for a swim with us in the Mediterranean' they said, 'the sea is warm now.'

The Chelebi led me into his study, and said: 'Now, is there anything you wish to ask me about the Order of Whirling Dervishes?

'Can you please explain the meaning of the posture held by the performer during the Whirling Dervish dance?' I said.

'The right arm is held up, with the palm open upwards, to

receive energy from the cosmos. The left arm and hand, pointing downwards, transmit this energy to the surrounding world.'

He then demonstrated the Whirling Dance, it was an unforgettable experience, which I can still recall, many years later.

His wife and two daughters entered the Study at that moment, and took me for a swim in the crystalline waters of the Mediterranean.

Such hospitality, extended to a stranger, is a rare quality which the Turks have cultivated, and made their own. It is demonstrated by their custom, during wedding festivities, of inviting a stranger in from the street to participate in the celebrations.

Although their thoughts and behaviour differ from my own culture, I was keenly aware of a common bond between us all.

This experience impelled me to return to Turkey many times, to participate in the Turkish way of life.

8. THE COMING OF PAK SUBUH

The Indonesian Mystic

'Pak Subuh will be coming to live at Coombe Springs, with his family and friends.'

The Leader's announcement was a surprise. We had heard that an Indonesian was coming to the West to introduce a new teaching. Pak Subuh - known to many as 'Bapak', was the founder of a spiritual teaching known as 'Subud'.

It was said that a ball of light, more brilliant than the sun, had appeared above him whilst he was walking with friends in Indonesia. This light seemed to enter him through his head, filling him with brightness. Many people had observed this phenomenon from a great distance.

Since Mr. Gurdjieff's death in 1949, we had continued to practise the exercises which he had transmitted to the Leader. In addition to this teaching, the Leader had introduced certain ideas of his own creation. We had been taught to practise sensation, relaxation, movements, awareness of thoughts, self-remembering, self-discipline, and the importance of the experience of 'I Am'.

I was standing outside the Djamichoonatra, awaiting the arrival of the Indonesians, with some trepidation. They walked gracefully, and with dignity, down the path, attired in colourful native costumes, and entered the unique building. I followed, then joined them, sitting cross-legged on the magnificent Eastern carpets which the Leader had brought from Turkey.

I noticed that Pak Subuh and his retinue were very relaxed, in comparison with us. Their bodies seemed to sink into the floor, as if they had no bones at all! I felt awkward in their presence. But they smiled gently, and made me feel at ease.

I sensed, instantly, that Pak Subuh possessed extraordinary powers. My first impression was that be had acquired an inner separation from the environment. It seemed that his emotions were completely hidden from the perceptions of the outer world. He emanated a quality of inner tranquillity, which I characterized as 'objective aloofness'.

From the beginning, I felt sure that his teaching was unsuitable for the West, and that it was primarily for his own culture. I thought that most of us were not sufficiently prepared to 'surrender to God', as demanded by Subud. Bapak claimed that the Latihan was a means of purification on the Path.

Before commencing the Latihan, men and women were segregated into separate rooms. We were then informed that we were going to be 'opened' by a 'Helper'.

I stood in front of the 'Helper' whilst this ritual was performed. I was not aware of any change in my organism. When the word 'begin' was uttered by the 'Helper', I closed my eyes, as instructed, and began the Latihan, which lasted for half-an-hour. I had been told that I could obey any impulse which arose within me.

Some women sobbed, others sang loudly, or screamed, or ran round the room. Yet others, like me, sat quietly, not knowing what to expect. The word 'finish' was eventually uttered by the 'Helper'.

After that first Latihan, I was told by the Leader 'to go and lie down'. But I did not wish to do so.

I practised the Latihan twice a week, as suggested by the Leader. I rarely felt an impulse to move, and sat with my eyes closed. I wondered if anything was happening to me

A few years later, I came upon a discourse by an Eastern teacher, dating back to the year 1150 A.D., who was widely acclaimed to be a Saint. He gave an astonishing description of the Latihan, with the most explicit warning not to practise it, on penalty of losing all possibility of real development.

Subud believes that man is a receptacle and transmitter of all kinds of forces, both animal and Divine. The Latihan is believed to be a process of purification for the individual, who will be slowly liberated from the dominance of lower energies.

Apart from the above explanations, which were offered to us by Bapak, there was no system of ideas in Subud, no practical instruction, and no teacher. Pak Subuh refused to give himself a title, but had no objection to being referred to as 'The Founder of Subud'.

Many of us were striving to understand how the Will of God worked within us. Some interpreted it in a completely passive manner. They waited for God to reveal all to them.

As Subud progressed, committees were formed to carry out various functions, and the original purity of the activity seemed to weaken. Some people tried to live as outlined in Pak Subuh's book, Susila Buddhi Dharma. This was the textbook which formed the suggested reading.

It seemed to me that there was a curious atmosphere of pretence surrounding those who were endeavouring to live according to the precepts outlined in Bapak's book. Members formed firm views as to how the practice of Subud should be organized, and which members should become 'helpers'. The latter was decided by what was known as 'testing', when a few 'helpers' assembled together, and decided by means of what was known as 'a spiritual communication', whether the person under consideration should join their ranks.

My beloved partner, Vasily, became an ardent follower of Bapak, and practised the Latihan regularly. I saw him less frequently, as he spent most of his time in the West Wing of the main house, where Bapak and his family resided. I knew that Vasily had strong religious feelings, perhaps because of his Russian ancestry.

One day, I was called to attend a 'testing' meeting. The 'helpers' were going to assess my suitability to become a 'Helper'.

'How would you feel if you surrendered to the Will of God?', one of them asked me.

Confronted with this unexpected question, I was overcome with nervous tension, wondering how I would feel if that experience should happen to me. Instead of falling to my knees, as the other pious ladies seemed to anticipate, I remained standing - apparently, a tense, trembling unbeliever!

I was surprised to discover, later, that I had been made a 'Helper - although I doubted that the decision was unanimous!

'Testing' included an attempt to discover the correct direction to take in one's life. A few members even emigrated to Australia, if the 'testing' so indicated.

Occasionally, people were 'tested' to discover whether their partners - or their marriages - were appropriate for them. If there was a negative 'response', they sometimes terminated the relationship.

Some people complained that they were unable to sleep in beds which had been occupied by non-Subud 'unfortunates',

A special Subud group was formed, known as '0' Group, which consisted of the most active and noisiest male members in the Latihan. These gatherings took place in a remote building in the grounds, located as far as possible from the house. Even so, the noise was appalling. Screams and shouts rent the air.

Certain people interpreted the injunction: 'Surrender to God' as a literal command, and waited for God to give them an indication. In doing so, they neglected the important advice from a sage: 'Trust in God - but tie your camel'.

As a result, there were a few casualties - some serious.

One of the members, Charles Gray, was an ardent follow-er of Subud, and attended the Latihans regularly. He appeared to be a normal, amiable, middle-aged business-man. One day, a member came to the office, and reported that Charles had started to perform the Latihan the previous day. Since then, he had shown no sign of stopping the exer-cise. We called some of his friends, who instantly went to his aid, and tried to persuade him to eat and drink.

But it was impossible to communicate with him. He appeared to be on another plane, and was not conscious on the ordinary, human level. Charles continued to perform the Latihan for several days, until he died of thirst and starvation.

I recall this period in the community as an uncomfortable experience for me. I never felt entirely at ease. Occasionally, when Pak Subuh's wife, Ibu, passed me in the main hall, she stuffed a handkerchief to her nose, and disappeared upstairs with her faithful ladies to perform the Latihan, leaving me with a vague sensation of being a sinner.

However, I discovered later that I was not alone in this feeling. Other women confided to me that they had had a similar experience. Ibu was a short, very plump woman, with eyes like shining black pools. Her expression - like Bapak's - was inscrutable.

I was sometimes asked to perform a Latihan with Eva Bartok, a well-known film actress. Our aims in life appeared to be the exact opposite. She had strong ambitions to go to Hollywood, and become a famous actress. I, on the other hand, had no particular ambition, but her ambition seemed to me to be absurd!

A year later, I received valuable practical help from Pak Subuh, at a time when I needed an objective view of my situation, relative to my possible marriage to Vasily, which now appeared to me to be unlikely.

One day, when I had reached a crisis of desperation about my relationship with Vasily, I ran up to Pak Subuh's apartment, and opened the door of his sitting room, which was normally reserved for male members. I asked the interpreter if I could speak with Pak Subuh. The room was filled with his male pupils. He immediately dismissed his companions, with a gesture of his hand.

He dealt with the situation as if he was already aware of what I wished to discuss with him. He showed me, with a few, well-chosen words, precisely where the problem lay and, at once, I knew what I should do.

'Pak Subuh' I said, 'I love Vasily, and he has promised to marry me, if I will bear his child. But, so far, I have not conceived. What can I do?'

Pak Subuh sat quietly for several minutes. Then he said, through his interpreter: 'Childbirth is not the most important reason for marriage. The love is more on your side than on his.'

I trusted his judgment. But his pronouncement was a bitter blow for me. I desired a child by Vasily. I desired it with every fibre of my being. No other man had ever aroused such feelings within me.

Shortly after this incident, Vasily told me that Pak Subuh had asked him to travel to Canada, where he had lived for some time during his earlier life. Pak Subuh had asked Vasily to introduce Subud throughout that country.

Vasily was destined to re-appear in my life, again and again, until his death in Las Vegas - his favourite city - in 2002, at the age of 84.

He was born in the Ukraine, of Russian-Jewish parents. The family had to flee from Russia when he was an infant.

They settled in Medicine Hat, Alberta, where he spent his childhood. Later, he took out American citizenship.

Many years later, I was told that Vasily had been a World War II pilot, and had taken part in the Battle of Britain. He never disclosed this part of his life to me. I only discovered it when he was visiting me, and suddenly realised that it was the anniversary of the deaths of some of his colleagues in the War. His experiences in that War probably accounted for his occasional depressions, and the fact that the door of his room always bore a design of a skull and crossbones, with the inscription: 'Memento Mori'.

Later, after Vasily had departed for Canada, John Bennett suggested that I might like to live with Eva Bartok at her White Cottage, near Coombe Springs. This I gratefully agreed to do. I knew that the only way to recover from the loss of Vasily, was to embark on a different course in my life.

There was an extraordinary woman living in the community, named Ethel Merston, whom I greatly admired. She lived in an ashram in India for six months of the year, and returned to the community for the remainder. She was tall and stately, and a true aristocrat. She wore a most incongruous garb: a sack-like garment enveloped the whole of her extensive frame. A pair of muli-strapped sandals covered her outsize feet.

She shuffled about like an amiable elephant, and wore a long pigtail. I guessed her age to be about 70. She was very eccentric, and there was always a sparkle in her eyes, as though she could sense something wonderful, which was hidden from the rest of us!

Ethel and I were always excluded by the Indonesians whenever special meetings were arranged. We wondered what the similarity between us was. On the surface, we appeared to be exact opposites: the dizzy blonde, and the eccentric aristocrat!

I discovered later that Ethel had participated in Gurdjieff's work at Fontainebleau in the 'twenties.

In 1958 Pak Subuh returned to Indonesia with his wife and his retinue. Some members continued to practice the Latihan in the community. It was at this time that I walked out of a Latihan, intending never to participate again in the exercise. Subud may have been an effective path for those who practised it in Indonesia. A few of the members appeared to have benefited by the practice of the Latihan at Coombe Springs.

I had no doubt that Pak Subuh was a man with remarkable powers. But I was seeking a different path, although I did not know at that time what form it would take.

9. INVITATION TO TEHRAN

Hilary Simpson was an adventurous woman who had travelled alone to Outer Mongolia, to discover something of the way of life of the natives of that culture.

I was delighted when she rang me, to suggest that I might like to spend a few weeks in her apartment on a nature reserve near the Elburz Mountains, beyond which lay the Caspian Sea.

I booked an Aeroflot flight to Tehran, via Moscow. It was a rare luxury to have caviar served with rich, dark brown Russian rye bread, accompanied by champagne, as we passed over Mount Ararat, at 3 a.m.

I was seated next to a charming American couple, who were dressed exactly alike, in woollen tweed trouser suits. I enjoyed their descriptions of their home in Santiago, where the temperature at Christmas was 78 degrees. Before the plane landed, they gave me their address, and an open invitation to visit them at any time.

We arrived in Tehran at 5am - one of the penalties of cheap air travel - and I curled up on a hard, wooden seat in the airport lounge. But the unfamiliar sounds of Farsi, together with the busy surroundings, and the excitement of arriving in a strange country, all tended to keep me awake , until I heard the sound of Hilary's voice greeting me.

We drove some miles out of the city, until we reached the magnificent region of the Elburz Mountains. Hilary's garden was exotic. Gaudily-coloured parrots flew around in profusion, and the legendary Hoopoe Bird was said to be nesting nearby. It was fluttering amongst the trees, flirtatiously revealing her gorgeous, vivid plumage, but never settling on the branches.

My friend's apartment was spacious, with a terrace overlooking the glorious mountains. We also enjoyed the luxury of air-conditioning.

It was difficult to visualise, in the sweltering heat of August that, in the winter, she skied on those same slopes.

The maid, who appeared to be a centenarian, glided noiselessly in and out of the dining room, placing before us delectable Persian dishes: meats cooked with fruit, and accompanied by succulent rice. The lamb was especially good here, but the water was boiled before drinking. The vegetables were soaked in permanganate of potash for half- an-hour, before cooking.

Breakfast was served on the terrace, where a gentle breeze, coming from the mountains, caressed our faces.

In these wonderful surroundings, I lost my sense of time. I realised that a week had passed. My nomadic nature was urging me to be on the move again.

Hilary had suggested a motoring trip to Isfahan. This idea entailed much preparation on her part, for she always prepared everything in great style. She provided blankets, an ice-box and various other items, every one of which proved to be necessary for the journey. This was a picnic de luxe!

We left early the next morning, whilst the sun was still low in the heavens. Hilary had planned to reach Isfahan that evening. Occasionally,we passed battered cars, piled up on the roadside, as a warning to motorists.

We stopped at an area of woodland, close to the road: we had to be careful to be within reach of protection, for our situation might become highly dangerous.

We protected ourselves from insect bites by lighting a number of cones. These emitted a substance that was highly unpleasant for insect life, especially the curious 'desert wasps', which were larger than their English counterpart, and had a 'catherine wheel' tail.

The picnic was elegant. It consisted of ham, melon and champagne - whilst we dangled our feet in a cool rivulet, running down from the mountains.

In the beautiful city of Isfahan, we visited the Friday Mosque, near the Maidane. But it was the month of the Fast of Ramadan, and it was apparent that women were not welcome in the Mosque. However, Hilary's knowledge of Farsi enabled us to enter, and to stay inside for a short period, which was sufficiently long to absorb the impact of the sublime architecture.

These surroundings affected not only my emotional state, but also my physical body. I had a strong sensation of being drawn upwards by the height and shape of the huge alcoves.

Later, I found a small print shop in the Maidane, and purchased a print of the interior of the Friday Mosque, and its alcoves. When I returned to England, I found that I could study the print, and retrieve the same sensation which I had experienced in the Mosque. That print was on my wall for many years, and eventually fell into tatters, after long appreciation.

One of the most remarkable buildings in Isfahan was the Abbas Abad Hotel. It was beautifully proportioned, and had been built for the Shah-in-Shah.

In the evening, we strolled in the picturesque gardens of the Hotel, and then sat, sipping green tea, in one of the lavishly-cushioned open lounges in the courtyard.

A wise-looking old gentleman was reading aloud in Farsi from an open book, placed on an ornate wooden lectern. Some of the men surrounding him were smoking the nargileh pipe.

Glancing up at the hotel windows, I noticed that they were designed in the style of the ancient caravansersi. Each window was domed, and lit from within. What a magnificent place for a honeymoon, I mused!

When we left the following morning, Hilary reminded me that it was my turn to drive. I was terrified. Huge trucks, approaching from the opposite direction, did not move into the correct lane until the last possible moment, confronting me with an alternative: to swerve into one of the numerous irrigation holes at the side of the road. These holes were often littered with wrecks of cars.

Much to my relief, we arrived safely back at the apartment.

But my thoughts were turning to the lands beyond the Caspian Sea. I was restless. The nature reserve was pleasant, but it was predominantly Western. I wanted to mingle with the native culture, despite the fact that I could not speak any of the languages in this part of the world. I had only ten days left, before my departure for London.

By a strange coincidence, I picked up a map lying on the table. I saw that there was a bus route out of Tehran, through the Elburz Mountains, and along the shores of the Caspian Sea, as far as Mashad. This was said to be a city inhabited by many fanatical Moslems, who disliked Westerners.

There appeared to be a local bus from Mashad to the Iranian frontier with Afghanistan. There was also a desert bus which regularly made the five-hour journey across the Afghan Desert to Herat.

I made a snap decision to go to Herat, despite my limited funds, and the short time left to me before my return to England. I reckoned that I would have to leave that evening on the overnight bus to Mashad.

A sinking sensation in my solar plexus reminded me that I needed an Afghan visa. I knew that the Afghan Travel Office was some distance away from the centre of Tehran. It was not possible to confer with Hilary, since she had left for her office in the city whilst the sun was still cool.

I took a bus to Ferdousi Avenue, and stood on the edge of the pavement, surveying the scene. There was an important building nearby, and I ran up the steps, and through the swing doors. A man, wearing a smart uniform, approached me. 'Seyffari Afghani?' I asked.

He replied in Farsi, but I did not comprehend. Then he disappeared, and returned some minutes later. 'I don't know' he said in stilted English.

I ran down the steps, and stood on the kerb.

'Seyffari Afghani!' I shouted to passing taxis. No one appeared to notice me.

I was giving up hope, when Providence came to my rescue, in the shape of a young Iranian man. 'You are standing on the wrong side of the road for Seyffari Afghani. Cross over, and try the other side.'

I crossed over, and yelled my message to passing traffic. Soon, a taxi stopped, and I got in, to discover that there were already six passengers, sprawled in various postures, sharing the vehicle with me. It stopped now and then to pick up additional fares.

After an exhausting journey, when I was squeezed so tightly that I could only breathe with difficulty, the driver stopped, and indicated to me to get out. He waved his hand vaguely towards a building nearby. I paid him, and began to look for the Travel Office. I soon spotted it.

I hurried past groups of hippies, all bound for Asia. Some were smoking pot. A friendly official immediately attended to me. 'You will need a photo for your visa,' he said. 'There is a photo shop round the corner.'

I was not going to be defeated at this late stage. I quickly discovered the shop, and within a few minutes I was the proud possessor of an Afghan visa. The official processed my papers swiftly. Within an hour, I was heading back in a taxi to the centre of the city.

The bus station in Tehran has no counterpart in the West. The huge entrance hall was crammed with 90 per cent males. Some wore colourful jellabas and turbans, others wore beautiful embroidered leather jackets and baggy trousers. Eyes of all shapes surveyed me: slanting, narrow, opium-drenched, wide brown eyes. All stared at me in astonishment.

The stench in the hall was assailing my nostrils, so that I could hardly bear to breathe it into my lungs!

I was a phenomenon: a blonde Western woman of uncertain age, alone, in this male predominance.

I sensed a mass energy in this crowd, which was frightening. I became uncomfortably aware that anything could happen, at any moment. I knew instinctively that I must keep a low profile, for my own safety.

'Never meet anyone's eyes' was a good maxim which I had learnt to use.

Here, the idea of queues was unknown. I knew, from experience, that in order to procure a ticket under these circumstances, a certain attitude was necessary. I flung a scarf around my head, tried to appear as nondescript as possible, and pushed my way forward to the front of the motley crowd, to where the bus official was standing. I knew that the traveller, despite a modest appearance, must also be aggressive, under these circumstances.

I shouted to the official: 'MASHAD!' I passed some notes to him, shouted a few words of Farsi, and he handed me a ticket.

I went out into the bus station yard with a sense of great relief. But there, to my dismay, I saw that none of the buses bore a destination.

It was then that I became aware of an extraordinary man standing near me. He was dressed very differently from the motley crowd in the hall. He wore a smart tweed jacket, grey flannel, well-cut trousers, and leather sandals. He was a striking man, with long black hair and bright blue eyes. He emanated a strong presence, and was outstanding amongst the crowd surrounding him. I thought that he might be an Afghan. I was sure that we shared no common language.

He seemed to realise my predicament, and pointed to a bus nearby. Somehow, I trusted this man with the powerful presence. I boarded the bus, and took a window seat.

I lit a cigarette and, glancing out of the window, saw my newly-found friend making amusing gestures, indicating that if I continued to smoke on the bus, the other passengers would begin to feel ill. I immediately stubbed out the cigarette in the little ash-tray fixed to the seat in front. The tray fell out, and stale cigarette ends and ash were scattered all over the bus floor.

Behind me, there was a loud dispute going on between a large Iranian woman and the driver. The argument became more heated, until she slapped the driver's face. Then everything became quiet. I thought that the argument might have been related to non-payment of fare.

Looking round the bus, I concluded that I was the sole Western passenger. Most of the people were travelling to the holy city of Mashad, to take part in ceremonies in the Mosque.

My new friend stood protectively outside my window, and began to paint hand pictures representing the panoramic scenes through which I would be passing, tracing the lakes, the mountains and the sea. I was beginning to hope that he would make the journey with me. But the wheels began to turn, and he waved goodbye to me with a warm smile.

The feeling I had as a result of this encounter lasted for most of the time I was on the bus, and gave me courage during the tiring overnight journey, which took eighteen hours. On arrival at Mashad, I found the connecting bus waiting for passengers for the frontier.

I quickly passed through the Customs formalities. The

Health officer remarked proudly: 'There is no disease here!'

It was 1978. The Soviet invasion of Afghanistan was imminent.

10. BEYOND THE CASPIAN SEA

Glimpses of Herat

At the Iranian frontier with Afghanistan, a trim, smartly clad official was standing nearby, wearing a suit the colour of the sand. 'Where is the minibus for Herat? I enquired.

'Round the corner' he answered, crisply.

I walked round the corner - and caught my breath at my first glimpse of the Afghan desert. I looked in all directions for the minibus, but no vehicle was visible through the desert haze. A soft breeze, coming off the desert, caressed my face. There was a rough path weaving into the distant sands. Slinging my airline bag over my shoulder, I took a chance, and followed the path. I had learnt to travel light on these occasions.

Presently, through the haze, an extraordinary sight met my gaze: an old minibus, surrounded by a motley, chattering crowd of men. Some wore rough garments made of sack-cloth; others wore exotic embroidered leather coats, baggy trousers and fur hats. I guessed that the latter had come from the Steppes of Central Asia. Some wore western clothes. No women were visible. The men were speaking in foreign tongues, and I listened in awe to the unfamiliar sounds.

The driver resembled a character out of 'The Arabian Nights': his skin had been burnt to a dusky brown by the desert winds. He wore a pristine, brilliant-white jellaba, which was flowing in the breeze. He had the profile of an eagle, and his head was adorned by a magnificent white tur-ban. He was unusual for a bus driver, I thought! He was middle-aged, but clambered tirelessly up and down to the roof-rack, depositing the travellers' luggage.

When the bustle had subsided, the driver turned to me, and indicated the seat beside him. I was fortunate, for the seating at the back was primitive, and consisted of hard wooden benches. The alternative was an expanse of solid, dirty wooden flooring in the centre of the bus.

We set off in a cloud of dust, and I settled down to a bumpy ride. But I had always loved the desert, and, although I knew that it was going to be a rough trip, I was not deterred. It would be at least five hours before we glimpsed the ancient ramparts of Herat. The bus was due to arrive at sunset.

I had a spectacular view of the desert. Far, far away, on the horizon, I glimpsed a herd of camels. At that great distance, they took on the appearance of toy gazelles, prancing about.

We passed small bands of musicians, sitting cross-legged on the sand, playing strange instruments; a small boy sat, singing, in the midst of the group. But, sadly, the music was inaudible inside the noisy, rattling old minibus.

An incongruous sight met my eyes as we sped across the sands. A small, square, brick building appeared, which seemed to be completely empty. A sign, painted in large letters on its side, bore the announcement:

THE BEST SMALL HOTEL

While we rattled across the great desert which separated Iran and Afghanistan, I listened to the conversation coming from the back of the bus. Most of it was incomprehensible to me, but I realised that there were a few English-speaking students from Israel, the Middle East, and Scotland.

I heard a familiar, Scottish accent coming from a pessimistic student, who was proclaiming to his colleagues: 'As soon as you eat or drink anything - you will be in hospital!'

I ignored such injunctions, for I was certain that they originated in the imagination of the speaker.

We were concerned about the condition of the old minibus, and wondered whether it had been serviced in the last ten years! It had come to a spluttering halt twice during the journey, but the indefatigable driver seemed to understand the engine, for it always responded to his efforts. I was nervous, for I had not seen any other vehicles since we started on our journey.

After two hours of uncomfortable rattling and bumping, the bus came to a halt The driver pointed to a chaihane, a crudely constructed wooden building. Inside, there were rough wooden tables and chairs - and very little light

All the precautions about food and drink had long been forgotten. We drank a strange-tasting Coca Cola. Then, we ventured to partake of kebabs and rice. It was delicious! We set off soon afterward, in order to reach Herat before darkness fell.

At sunset, the ramparts appeared, starkly silhouetted against the sunlight. We drove through the outskirts of the historic city, which was on the route of the old Silk Road from China. Picturesque maidanes adorned the route, until, finally, we entered the walled courtyard of a small hotel.

My room was simply furnished, with a bed and cupboard. But a bed was all I needed at that moment in time! I sank, exhausted, into a deep, refreshing sleep.

I awoke at 6am, eager to explore the city. In the distance was the Citadel, the ancient ruins of buildings dating back thousands of years. It had a rich, golden hue which is characteristic of stonework dating from a forgotten age. I wanted to explore the structure, but a passer-by intimated that the ruins were inhabited by snakes.

There were many small shops and stalls in the market;

some were mere holes-in-the- wall, artistically draped with wares of all descriptions. Fur coats, fashioned from the local fox, were displayed around the walls, priced at the equivalent of £20! In another shop, there were hand-made leather boots, at a lower price than any I had seen in the West

I gazed longingly at bangles and rings, set in lapis lazuli and cornelian. Above it all, there wafted the subtle perfumes of fragrant spices.

Some shopkeepers invited me into their small alcoves, and offered me a cup of special green tea, which is drunk in Afghanistan. I learned a little about their way of life, as most of them spoke some English.

A young Afghan man told me that he and his colleagues were discontented with the marriage laws in his country. He told me: 'If, and when I wish to get married, I shall have to ask my father to choose a bride for me. Even then, I shall not be permitted to see the face of my spouse until after the ceremony!'

I had found a comfortable, modern hotel in the centre of the city. I had a pleasant room, which was furnished in carved oak, with hanging cupboards complete with locks, and a private bathroom - all for £2 a night!

From my veranda, I could sit and watch the passers-by and the life of the city.

At the edge of the city, too, I had found a seat where I could sit and watch a fascinating scene unfolding before me. A caravanserai was arriving on the old Silk Road from China, after a long journey through the desert. The women were completely veiled by a burqa, a thin silk, full-length garment, with myriad pleats falling from the head-piece. Inside the garment, there was a kind of face-mask. I thought this might make it difficult for them to see - or even to breathe! The men were handsome, and rode their camels with great dignity. At the rear, a herd of camels was laden with merchandise.

The men wore exotic clothing: embroidered silk waist-coats, with full, swathed silk trousers, as well as full-length, multi-coloured silk coats. Long, coloured silken panels hung from the backs of their coats, which enhanced their dignity.

There was a medieval quality about life in this city, which contrasted strongly with the tensions of Western life. It was as if I had stepped back through centuries, for there was an absence of stress here. Carriages took the place of cars - there were scarcely any motor vehicles. No one hurried, and, observing people in the streets, there was a striking feature in the way they walked. They appeared to be aware of their bodies, and living in the present moment. I reflected that, in the West, people were often distracted from the quality of life in the present moment. They were troubled by anxiety about the past, or the future.

It was Sunday afternoon, and from my veranda I watched Afghan families passing by in gaily painted, horse-drawn carriages. This seemed to be their favourite way of spending Sunday afternoons.

There were no cars on the roads. Occasionally, an Afghan man cycled slowly past, on his way home, wearing baggy trousers, a turban and a sports jacket A solitary truck drove by, brightly painted with gay floral designs.

I discovered that traders were not interested in making much profit from their wares. They needed only sufficient money to keep themselves fed and clothed; there was little concern with competition, so they were more able to manifest their own individuality.

Evenings in Herat were memorable. From my veranda, I had a view of the long road leading to the great Mosque. When darkness fell, the street lighting was dimmer than in the West. But the effect was charming. Lights twinkled here and there on the road, fading away into darkness at the far end, where lay the Mosque.

I did not venture out alone at night, but on my veranda I listened to the beautiful sounds of an Afghan singer, said to be the most popular vocalist in Afghanistan; people paid high prices for his recordings. The singing was broadcast to the city from a building in the main street It was unlike any other music I have ever heard,

One evening, I was visited by some students with whom I had travelled on the minibus. They were obviously intrigued by the idea of a Western woman travelling alone in countries like Iran and Afghanistan. I told them that I merely followed a few, simple rules while travelling, and these seemed to be effective.

1.   Keep a low profile.
2.   Never look into anyone's eyes.
3.   Have just a little faith that all will be well.

These simple rules had helped me to venture into the unknown.

'Come with us to a café. We ate there yesterday, and the food was good.'

They took me to a small chaihane in the main street. The cook, attired in a white jellaba and white turban, was frying meat balls in a huge, smoking frying-pan. We went inside, and sat on long, wooden benches. The walls were covered with very old photographs of attractive Afghan men and women.

The smoke from the frying-pan was blowing back into the dining-room, and my eyes began to water. But when the food eventually arrived, it was delicious: luscious meat-balls made with young minced lamb, cooked with Afghan spices, and delicious Basmati rice.

I was planning to leave the next morning, as I had a tight travel schedule. I had to arrive in Tehran in three days' time, in order to catch my plane to London via Moscow. The daily desert bus departed for the Iranian border at 6am.

When I arrived at the bus stop the following morning, a few minutes before it was due, I was dismayed to discover that it had already left for the border! My mind started racing around: I imagined myself marooned in Herat, penniless. For not only was I travelling on a tight schedule. I was also travelling on a tight budget. I counted my cash, and realised that I would not have sufficient to pay the bus fare from the frontier to Tehran. In 1978, there were no facilities for obtaining cash from banks in that region. Most of the people were poverty-stricken.

The alternative was to take a taxi across the desert to the border with Iran. But that would cost much more than the bus fare. I decided to take a taxi. In reality, I had no choice; remaining in Herat in a penniless condition was not a feasible alternative.

A taxi was waiting, and I hailed it. As we sped across the desert, I was thankful that the journey was more comfortable, and more speedy, than the bus. But there was little relief in that reflection, for I had to think fast about my financial predicament. I had budgeted carefully, but had not allowed for unexpected expenses.

I arrived in good time at the Frontier, to catch the local bus to Mashad. I had just sufficient cash to pay the driver. But, now, I was faced with another problem. The bus to Mashad had been cancelled. I knew, from past experience of travelling in foreign parts, that the surest way of getting assistance was to ask for it! So I started talking to a few men near me, trying to make myself understood. I explained that I had to be in Tehran by Monday, and it was now Saturday.

The word had got around! In a few minutes a small boy ran up to me and shouted: 'Truck leaving now, arriving Tehran tomorrow morning!'

This was incredibly fortunate. I went outside to inspect the truck-driver, and to assess whether the situation seemed safe. It did. He was Turkish, and did not understand English. He was well-dressed, and seemed to be quite respectable. He motioned to me to get into the cockpit. I learned later that he was transporting a diplomat's home to Tehran.

Soon, we were driving along the short distance to the Afghan and Iranian Customs office. I noticed, with alarm, that there were many trucks awaiting Customs inspection. How could we possibly get away in time to reach Tehran tomorrow? I could not induce my driver to understand the reasons for my anxiety - or, indeed, to understand anything! Presently, we were joined by an elderly Pakistani, with bright, brown eyes, who spoke English.

'You are not going to get away from here today' he said, 'You must leave the truck altogether, and stay in Taipan, a nearby village. You must attempt to get to Mashad, and then to Tehran, in some other way. You will have difficulty in getting to Taipan, as there are no taxis, and it is approached by a mile-long road cut through the desert. There are no street lights.'

Dusk was falling. But I continued to be fortunate. The Pakistani, who was also going to stay in Taipan, had a friend with a car. I was driven to a small hotel, and collected by the same driver in the morning, and then driven to the frontier.

I sat on a seat at the edge of the desert. Looking out over the sands, I could see no buses, and wondered how I was going to get to Mashad.

Suddenly, in my desperation, an idea occurred to me: I had purchased a beautiful embroidered leather coat in Herat, which I was wearing. It was a purchase which I could ill-afford, but could not resist. Now, I was going to attempt to sell it, which should provide sufficient funds for a bus ticket to Tehran - and leave a little cash for buying food.

I took off the coat, and laid it on the desert. This would indicate to the strange characters standing around, that I wished to bargain with them. They were accustomed to bargaining!

They certainly bid for the coat, but the bids were only for half its real value. In my situation, I could not afford to let it go for less than its real value.

News suddenly came through - as news always does in these parts - that a bus would soon be leaving for Mashad. I got a seat on it, and began to feel that I was now moving in the right direction, although I had lost half a day at the border - time that was precious to me.

I arrived in Mashad early Sunday afternoon, and knew that I must get away before nightfall, in order to reach Tehran by Monday. There would be sufficient time, there, to have a sleep at Hilary's apartment, have a meal, and proceed to the airport to board the plane for Moscow.

I went to the ticket office, and enquired about the evening bus to Tehran. 'No, the evening bus is full!' was the curt rejoinder.

I pleaded with the bus official, and explained my situation. He understood English. 'One ticket for tonight's bus: 550 dinars!' he shouted.

The cost of this journey was much higher than the outward trip, but I was learning that prices here varied from day to day! I had only 200 dinars, and showed him the notes.

He bent forward, and fingered a beautiful amber pendant which I was wearing.

'For this' he said, 'I give you ticket to Tehran!'

To my Western mind, the idea was preposterous! 'No!' I said firmly

I now realised that it was essential for me to sell my coat. I walked to what appeared to be the centre of the city; it was an ancient street, and some of the paving stones were broken or displaced. I had to keep my eyes firmly on the pavement, to avoid falling. I noticed a street corner which seemed to be suitable. I laid out the coat on the pavement, and waited. It was the month of the Fast of Ramadan, and in Mashad, people were not friendly to Westerners.

Bu the passers-by were showing some interest in the garment. A crowd began to gather round, and the bargaining began. After a few bids, it was clear to the crowd that I was not going to sell the coat for less than its real value. One of the men suddenly called out the price I needed. I quickly handed him the coat, took the cash, and hurried back to the bus station.

Approaching the same official, I showed him the notes. He took the money, and said: No ticket - but place on bus tonight!'

No ticket! I thought - just a place on the bus tonight! This was unbelievable. I saw that I now had to take this man on trust I had given him my precious money, and now, I had no choice left - in this town, where hardly anyone understood English.

I took a seat in the bus station. I was divided between a feeling of despair, and the faith that everything would turn out well. It seemed to me, then, that I was in the hands of Fate, and that I could do nothing further, of my own volition.

Now and then, a little Iranian boy approached me, and offered me a sweet from his bag. This was a delightful, human gesture in the midst of uncertainty.

Time passed slowly. I was inwardly affirming my intention to get on that bus! Someone suddenly ran in, shouting: 'Bus leaving for Tehran now! Two seats left!'

There was no way that I was going to miss that bus! I boarded it firmly, not looking to left or right. The driver did not ask me for my ticket, and said nothing.

As we drove out of the bus station, a crowd outside was shouting: 'Let us get on!'

They were hippies, stranded in Mashad. The driver shouted: 'Yes - for 1000 dinars!' They were left, to spend another night in Mashad

I was surrounded by a number of Moslem women; they were devout Shias, and were commemorating the martyrdom of Mohammed's son-in-law and his sons. The driver, who was the husband of the woman sitting beside me, began to chant loudly, and the Shias responded each time he uttered the words. This continued for fifteen minutes; the women were weeping and wailing, with tears streaming down their cheeks. It seemed as though they were actually experiencing the intense suffering of the martyrs.

Afterwards, everyone seemed to realise that there was a foreigner in their midst - although I had tried to keep a low profile, and bent my head during the commemoration.

The woman beside me wiped away her tears, and smiled warmly behind her yashmak. She offered me some food. I learnt that one of the tenets of Islam permitted Moslems to eat whilst travelling.

There were a number of stops on the route. I noticed that the women behaved in a sisterly way towards me, and always invited me into cafes. They insisted that I should share a large dish of food with them, eating with one hand, as is their custom. Our sign-language was quite effective - perhaps it was more direct than words. I felt a strong connection with them, as I have always felt, when in the company of Moslems.

We ate our last meal in a café near the Elburz Mountains, and the Caspian Sea. In the early morning light, we washed our hands in a running stream, before continuing our journey to Tehran.

I arrived at Hilary's apartment at lunch-time. She was astonished to hear of my adventures, which I related whilst she was preparing a meal for me. She then drove me to the airport, as my plane was due to depart for Moscow in a few hours.

Little did I know that the small print on the back of my Aeroflot airline ticket, specified that it was a provisional booking, and that I should have rung Aeroflot to confirm it.

I had to wait until the last passenger had boarded the aircraft, before claiming my seat.

11. THE DOMAIN OF THE DESERT

Tangier is a fascinating city. It is the gateway to many beautiful regions of Morocco. I wanted to explore a very different part of the country, which lay beyond the High Atlas Mountains.

I discovered that a bus travelled up the perilous slopes of the High Atlas, through the Tizi n'Tichka Pass - the highest mountain pass in Morocco - ending its journey at Ouazazate, a small oasis in the Sahara Desert.

'You sit there!' shouted the driver. I took the window seat and settled down amidst a motley crowd of passengers.

The old bus set off from Taroudant to follow the long, arduous route to Ouazazate. In the back of the vehicle a mountain farmer was endeavouring to control his unruly lamb. A plump Berber woman, sitting behind me, was blissfully breast-feeding her infant On the other side of the bus, an unhealthy-looking man, with a sallow skin, wearing a brown woollen djellaba, was quietly vomiting into a tin.

This was the way I preferred to travel, surrounded by the people of the culture. I did not consider myself a tourist, and felt strangely at home in these surroundings.

These men and women differed from the cosmopolitan crowd in Tangier. I was eager to learn more about their tribal way of life.

The travellers were Bedouin and Berber. Some were farming in the High Atlas, others travelling to join their families in the desert. I was curious to learn about their lives under those conditions.

As the bus continued its long, dangerous climb to the

summit, the rough road became increasingly narrow. The driver frequently negotiated hazardous hairpin bends, with a precipitous drop on one side. He was travelling at high speed, and invariably sounded the horn at treacherous points. But the warning was inaudible on the other side of the bend, due to the speed of the vehicles, the density of the rock, and the clatter of the ageing buses. Every time we approached a blind bend, I held my breath, and felt certain that we would never attain the summit, but would be hurled on to the rocks below.

The path was too narrow for vehicles to pass easily. They stopped constantly, to allow oncoming traffic to navigate the dangerously narrow bends.

The precipice on the left afforded a spectacular view of the desert. But, to my horror, there was also the terrifying sight of wrecked vehicles strewn across the mountainside!

The bus stopped at small villages, where storks were nesting on the roofs of houses. Every year, they each returned to their respective house.

The women of the mountains were bold, wide-eyed and flamboyant. They wore glittering, dangling earrings. They were unlike the women of Tangier, who revealed no more than beautiful dark eyes, glimpsed through narrow slits in their yashmaks. These women took great pride in their appearance and wore bright colours, flaunting their femininity.

The journey up the mountain ended abruptly at the summit. There was a stunning view of the sun setting on one side, whilst the moon was rising on the opposite horizon.

The bus suddenly emerged from the peaks, to be confronted with a dazzling vista of golden sand, covered with glittering quartz. We were descending into the Sahara Desert. A herd of wild camel was browsing in the far, far distance. There was an extraordinary sense of peace. I wanted to remain here, to absorb its unique magic. But we were approaching Ouazazate.

It was 1969. At that time, the oasis consisted of a single-track path leading out into the desert. There were a few ramshackle buildings, seemingly unoccupied, and, incongruously, a Club Méditerranée. I knew that the latter would not provide the experiences which I sought: contact with the people of the desert.

As I got off the bus, I noticed that there were no women in the Street. Until that moment, I had been captivated by the panorama surrounding me. I suddenly realized that it was late afternoon, the sun was setting in this remote place - and I had nowhere to stay. I had no knowledge of the languages spoken in this part of Morocco.

The men standing at the bus stop stared curiously at me - not without reason. A solitary, blonde Western woman of uncertain age, arriving alone at this remote oasis, was certain to attract attention.

One of the onlookers approached me. He had the appearance of a benign, elderly man. His face was burnt dark brown with sun and wind. His eyes had a kindly expression. 'You come stay my family' he said.

I hesitated. In this country, I had learned to be wary of invitations from strangers. I looked closely at him, and, instinctively, felt that I could trust him.

At that moment, exhaustion overcame me, and I answered, wearily: 'Sokran (thank you). I will come with you.'

I followed him down the shabby path, which served as a main street, until we reached the edge of the desert. It was August, and the heat was intense.

'I am Ibrahim Siddidout,' he said. He gestured vaguely towards some sand dunes, and remarked: 'My family live in that house over there'.

I could not see a dwelling anywhere. My heart began to

pound rapidly. Suddenly, I realized that I was alone with this stranger, whose language and customs I did not comprehend. Night was falling.

What was going to happen to me?

Ibrahim calmly motioned to me to step off the dusty path, and I followed him some distance across the sands. Soon, I noticed in the distance, a primitive dwelling emerging from the desert haze. It had no doors or windows, and there was no roof. It was constructed of mud and straw.

'This is my house' said Ibrahim, proudly.

There was no alternative. I stepped through the arched aperture, which served as a front door, into one of the partitioned rooms.

Ibrahim handed me a small rug, which I learnt to carry with me in the house, on which I could sit in any room in which I chose to settle.

Ibrahim's wife, Tuda, emerged from the dark interior. She was a tall, handsome woman, and wore glittering earrings and bangles, and a brightly-coloured long silken dress, which suited her nubile form. Her movements were graceful. But her skin was rough, and her thin body indicated to me that she was suffering from malnutrition.

The only language we shared was a strange version of French, which they had learned from a French regiment operating in the vicinity. They spoke a few words of English, which they had probably learned from tourists.

I had come to the desert during the hottest, most unsuitable month for Westerners, and spent part of the day sleeping on a crude, but clean, mattress. It was impossible to remain awake in the intense heat of the afternoon, so I took refuge in slumber. Occasionally, I awoke to find their two children standing, staring at me, as if I was a being from another planet. Perhaps they had never seen a blonde woman before.

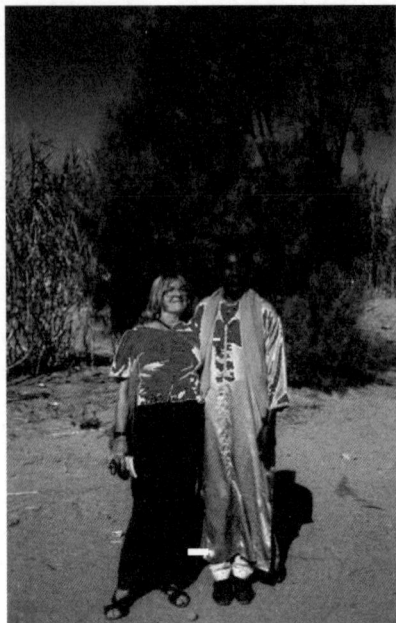

Photos from a later visit to Morocco:
Helena and Touda at Ouazazate
Rue de la Plage, Tangier

Garden well

Gateway to Sirdar Iqbal Ali
Shah's house

At mealtimes, Tuda secreted herself in a dark corner of the room, and cooked lamb on a charcoal burner. It was her custom to serve meat only lightly cooked. But the lamb was young and tender, and served with luscious rice. I took a risk, and ate it. In these surroundings, the dangers of eating partially-cooked meat never affected me, and I did not suffer any ill-effects.

Tuda always performed a ritual before we began to eat. She produced an old copper kettle, filled with water, and demonstrated to me how to rub my hands together, whilst she slowly poured water upon them. This was a cleansing ritual, which I always enjoyed.

Every morning, Tuda and I walked across the desert to the local well. She balanced a large ewer upon her head, and walked gracefully to the watering place near the well, where all the local desert women were assembled. It seemed to be a communal centre, where they chatted and laughed together. It was an exclusively feminine venue.

At nightfall, the family and I climbed the rickety stairs to the open terrace above, carrying our mattresses. I lay, listening to the fascinating sounds of distant drums and chanting in the desert, where sounds carry great distances.

Later in the night, a marvellous peace descended upon the desert.

I stayed for some days with Tuda and Ibrahim. We lived what some people would consider a primitive form of existence. But there was a quality of life here which I had not found anywhere else, despite the obvious poverty which was endured by the family.

Ibrahim worked in a large building behind the oasis. Local people referred to it as 'the great building'. I understood that it was the chief source of employment for the fortunate men who managed to obtain a job in the factory, where tyres were manufactured.

One morning I walked alone into the desert. I had discovered that if there was a breeze the sand dunes shifted, and the desert landscape took on a different form. On this particular day, I was completely lost. It was a frightening experience. Fortunately, though, a French army Land-Rover patrol spotted me, and drove me back to the dwelling of Tuda and Ibrahim.

On another occasion, when I was strolling down the main street, I was alarmed to see a huge black cloud approaching me. It was a whirlwind! A Bedouin, standing near me, indicated, by his bodily gestures, how to protect myself from the storm. He folded his arms in front of his eyes, and turned his back to the oncoming whirlwind. I imitated his movements, and the storm swept past me, disappearing into the desert

The time had come for me to bid farewell to the Berber family. When I offered some dirhams to cover the expenses of my stay with them, they refused to accept the money, and said: 'Tell your friends in England to visit us!'

I doubted that any of my acquaintances would wish to follow in my eccentric footsteps.

I was sorry to leave these simple, hospitable people, who had introduced me to a completely different way of life. During my brief stay with Tuda and Ibrahim I had sensed, in their daily lives, a simple faith,

which gave me an insight into the meaning of religion. Something radiated from these people, despite their poverty and their hard lives. I had experienced a similar sensation whilst living in the native quarter in Tangier. There seemed to be a thread running through their lives together, which connected them with a common purpose.

12. ST PANCRAS - MURMANSK

I was scanning the travel columns of a Sunday newspaper, when an unusual announcement caught my attention:

SEE THE MIDNIGHT SUN!

MEET THE REINDEER MEN!

My latent desire for adventurous travel was stimulated. I felt a need to travel again in foreign parts, and rang the agency. A pleasant, North-country accent greeted me. They were offering a journey by coach to Budapest. A Russian train would then take the tourists to St. Petersburg, where they would spend a few days, before setting off for Murmansk - the largest city in the Arctic Circle.

I made a snap decision to go. The cost, for more than two weeks, was moderate, and all-inclusive.

When the coach arrived at St. Pancras, I was surprised to find that it was already half- full of passengers from the North, who had boarded it in Lancashire.

I was seated next to a portly East European gentleman, who had secreted a bottle of whisky in his breast pocket, and frequently imbibed some of its contents. The strong odour began to permeate our corner of the vehicle.

It was an economy coach, and the seating was too narow for comfort. My neighbour, because of his immense girth, occupied part of my seat in addition to his own!

The lady behind, who appeared to be quite normal, leant forward and whispered to me: 'I am suffering from acute claustrophobia!'

A party of Welshmen, at the back, insisted upon conversing in their own language, so it was impossible to communicate with them.

It was 1982, and we were living in the pre-Glasnost era.

One of the passengers suddenly stood up, and announced proudly, in ringing tones: 'I am a communist!'

It had never occurred to me that the tour might have been organized by the communist organization. But it soon became apparent that the tour leader, whose name was Carl, was an ardent communist from the Party in the north of England. He was anxious to indoctrinate us, whenever possible. But we were hard to convince, and reacted light-heartedly to his diatribes. We greeted his outbursts with good-humoured scepticism.

When he began to expound on the subject of communism, one passenger remarked loudly: 'Now begins Chapter One.'

The leader appeared to be impervious to our reactions. 'I purchased a large mansion in Yorkshire, some years ago,' he said, 'for only ten thousand pounds. It is now valued at four million pounds - but I can only afford to insure it for one million.'

What an advertisement for communism, I thought. His remarks later confirmed the observations which I made while travelling in Russia: communism was for the elite. I saw wealthy Russians shopping in the exclusive gift stores, where only dollar and sterling currencies were accepted. The Russian man-in-the-street was, literally, begging a Western visitor to buy him a packet of American king-size cigarettes from the forbidden shop, for which he was willing to pay more than their value, in roubles.

During a break for refreshment, Carl produced a china mug. On it was inscribed a picture of his mansion in the north of England. The caption read 'LABOUR'S HOME'

He was a slim man in his seventies. He wore a well-cut, light grey suit, and had an extraordinary command over his body, remaining alert, although he managed with very little sleep.

I thought that his strong belief - his dedication to communism - was a source of energy for him. At times, he appeared to be utterly exhausted, but had a will to persist, despite difficulties.

'I travel to many countries by coach, train or plane,' he said. 'I must be the most-travelled man in the United Kingdom.'

The journey was tedious - I was uncomfortable, and could not sleep. At last, we arrived in Budapest. The woman behind me leant forward and whispered: 'Let's go in search of a bar, and find some good Hungarian wine.'

There was a two-hour wait, before the Russian train departed for St. Petersburg. We pooled our limited linguistic resources, but, alas! the language defeated us. Our search culminated in a glass of unpalatable sherry.

Our train was waiting. It stretched away into the far distance, and I saw the magical words: BUDAPEST - LENINGRAD, engraved upon the side of the carriage.

There were four bunks in each compartment. I quickly secured a top bunk, for I had heard that bottom bunks were uncomfortable on Russian railways, due to the lurching of the trains.

Life on the train was a challenge. I shared a compartment with a married couple, and a lady from Lancashire, whose voice, though similar to that of Gracie Fields, lacked the musical resonance of that famous star.

There was an art in preparing for sleep - and this art had to be learned. The husband discreetly disappeared in the direction of the washroom, whilst the ladies donned their night attire, with difficulty, in such a limited space. We took turns to use the toilet-cum-washroom at the end of our carriage. There, conditions were exasperating. The water tap was operated by a lever at its side, which had to be pressed upward, whereupon a jet of water squirted out on to one hand, while the other hand pressed the lever. There was no plug for the basin.

Brushing my teeth was such a complicated operation that I eventually gave up, in despair.

In our party, one of the men had lost a leg in the Spanish Civil War. I was curious as to how he contrived to operate the complicated washing and toilet facilities, since it was necessary to hold on to a stable object, due to the constant lurching of the fast-moving train.

The bunks were comfortable, with good mattresses and thick blankets, but they were too narrow: a restless sleeper on a top bunk risked a bad fall if they suddenly turned over, in the wrong direction, in their sleep.

On the first night I was dreaming, and had a nightmare. I shrieked, and my cry awoke the man on the opposite bunk. He assumed, in his half-waking state, that his wife had been disturbed on her bunk below, and, tuning over quickly, fell to the floor, sustaining a bad bruise to his shoulder.

During the journey, it was essential to practise some form of physical exercise, and I adjourned every morning to the end of the carriage, to practise deep breathing and body bends. The porter, who had his little office and kitchen there, and slept in the adjoining compartment, approved of my physical efforts, and looked on, smiling benignly. He was a dour-faced, blue-eyed man, with a severe expression. He brewed strong Russian tea on a charcoal burner, which he served to us in samovars, several times during the day. It was fragrant, and greatly enjoyed by all.

One evening, I was lying on my bunk, having a late-night conversation with the man on the opposite bunk, before settling down to sleep.

'The situation in Afghanistan is becoming very serious,' he remarked.

'Yes,' I replied, 'it was a great pity that Russia invaded that country!'

An indignant female voice, with a pronounced North-country accent, floated up from the bottom bunk: 'Russia never enters any country, unless that country requests her to do so!'

At that moment, I turned over, and fell asleep.

The next morning, I was conversing with the tour leader. 'Why don't you live in Russia,' I asked, 'since you obviously prefer the Russian way of life?'

'I am determined to stick it out in England,' he replied, 'because of my desire to promote my beliefs - although it is a most difficult task.'

'I am not interested in politics,' I said sharply, trying to veer the conversation away from his favourite topic.

'But politics is interested in you,' he said, with a fanatical glint in his eyes.

I refrained from further comment.

Our meals on the train were excellent. They were served in the dining-car, ten carriages away. We staggered over the dangerous couplings, four times a day, passing through the squalid quarters occupied by poorer Russians who, unlike us, did not have the benefit of sliding doors sealing off their sleeping quarters. They were provided with only a small table on which to prepare their meals. They could not afford to eat in the dining car. They cast resentful glances at us, and we tried to avoid embarrassing them, by looking straight ahead as we filed past.

Food had assumed an exaggerated importance. Breakfast consisted of three fried eggs, slices of cheese, and lots of delicious Russian dark brown rye bread, and butter. Good coffee was plentiful, and excellent beer was served at lunch and supper. We looked forward to our meals with relish.

During the day, I noticed that the Russians' favourite way of passing the day was to lie on their bunks, reading, or sleeping. Some of us acquired their habits, from boredom with the scenery, which was becoming monotonous, consisting of miles of fir forests. Fortunately, there was a radio in each compartment

The train stopped at several small country stations, and I got off to mingle with the country folk. There was a small wooden hut on the platform, which sold everything from gramophone records and carved wooden pencils, to ice cream and coloured photographs of the famous Russian circus. They cost only a few kopeks.

Buxom women passed me, carrying baskets filled with locally-grown berries, which I could not identify. Men hurried past, on their way home, wearing cream-coloured caps and high boots, a favourite form of apparel in the country. A wide-faced countryman, wearing a blue cap, which exactly matched his eyes, embraced a plump woman with great passion and almost brutal delight!

The porters were usually smart young women, wearing red-peaked caps and neat blouses, with knee-length skirts. They gave an efficient atmosphere to the railway stations.

Suddenly, there was a great commotion. We had arrived at St Petersburg. A coach took us to a smart high-rise hotel on the outskirts of the city.

There were three single women on the tour, including myself. We were allocated a large communal room with an en suite bathroom, on the fourteenth floor. This room became known as 'the English ladies' room'.

When I am in a foreign country, I prefer to explore the terrain alone. If I travel with a companion, I have to give some attention to them. But, when I am alone, I have more spare attention to observe my surroundings.

The following morning, I took a tram to the centre of the city. As I got on, I put three kopeks into the hand-operated slot-machine, and turned a handle, to obtain a ticket. Public transport is cheaper in Russia than in most other countries.

I searched in my Russian-English dictionary for the equivalent of 'camera repair shop'. A man on the opposite side noticed my predicament, and came over to sit beside me. I looked at him closely. He had a wide, open face with large blue eyes, of the colour which one finds only in Russia. I decided that he was OK.

I pointed to the word 'camera', with its Russian equivalent, and together we worked out the directions to a camera shop in Nevsky Prospekt.

When we got off in the historic square leading to the Prospekt, he led me to the camera shop, then bade me a warm farewell, with a delightfully flowery speech, as he knew some words of English. He looked up another Russian phrase in the dictionary - the equivalent of 'to be of assistance', said goodbye, and disappeared.

My camera was Japanese, and the shop dealt only with Russian equipment.

I walked the length of the Prospekt, and explored it at my leisure. It stretches for three miles, and is three times wider than London's Oxford Street

I gazed at the many different faces passing by: black-haired men, with fiery black eyes and long, black beards, which reminded me of Rasputin. There were fair-haired men, with high cheek-bones and blue eyes, and a vigorous, healthy appearance. I passed slim, dark-haired women, often very beautiful, whom I guessed came from Georgia. There were slant-eyed, Mongolian faces, with faintly yellow skin.

All passed in a motley throng. Some were eating ice cream, for which there were long queues. Here, it is considered to be a great delicacy. Russians consume it all the year round - even when snow is deep on the ground.

When I was chatting with Carl, I remarked that I was very fond of ice cream.

'I will take you to the finest ice cream parlour in St

Petersburg,' he said, proudly. There was a long queue in the parlour, but he pushed his way swiftly to the front, explaining, in fluent Russian, that he had little time to spare before returning to the coach. The assistant weighed out ice cream on a pair of scales, serving each customer with half a pound. We sat in Victorian, crimson velvet upholstered armchairs, devouring our huge mounds as elegantly as possible, in the short time left to us. It was the most delicious ice cream I had ever tasted.

The Russians take a very poor view of what is termed 'ice cream' in the West!

It is difficult to identify shops in Russia, if you have no knowledge of the language. They rarely have a window display, except for large department stores.

I discovered some intriguing interiors. I joined a queue, ignorant of what lay behind the double doors. It was a self-service cafeteria in a basement, seemingly patronized only by Russian males. I felt out of my depth, but decided to stay. I need not have worried: no one appeared to notice me.

I poured a cup of coffee from a large urn, and served myself with an exotic dish from an adjoining kitchen. It was piled high with fresh cream, mixed with cream cheese and chopped fruit, and a few other delicacies which I could not identify.

The cost, for such good quality food, was very reasonable! But there were no tables or chairs, merely a long counter, at which diners stood, enjoying their repast, whilst reading their Pravdas.

I stopped in the street, in the hot sunshine, to queue for a plastic cup of spring water, served at a little stall, for five kopeks.

I found a grocery shop - unrecognisable from the exterior. The counters were adorned with stylish Victorian lamps, shaped in the form of glass tulips, illuminating bowls of salted fish.

Stocks of food were scanty. A stall was piled high with bananas, and a long queue formed. But the fruit rapidly disappeared, and the crowd remaining had to wait for the next consignment.

St. Petersburg is a beautiful city - built for giants. Its streets are so long that the end disappears in a kind of haze. Such overwhelming space had an exhilarating effect upon me.

Parts of the city, near the river Nev, had been designed by a Scotsman, named Campbell, in the 17th Century. He had lived in Italy for some years, and was influenced by Venetian architecture. Some of the small bridges, and parts of the waterway, were almost identical with some areas of Venice

Certain parts of the city were in need of repair. Broken pavements were a relic of German shelling during the Second World War. A plaque in Nevsky Prospekt commemorated the War.

A large, beautifully proportioned church in a street off the Prospekt, was adorned with stained glass windows. It had been closed for ten years.

There was a 'dollar shop' in the Prospekt, which sold expensive china tea sets and many other high quality goods, including American king-size cigarettes. The Russian man in the street, who possessed only roubles, was forbidden to shop there, since they accepted only dollar or sterling currencies.

I was walking in Nevsky Prospekt, when a Russian man approached me, and asked, in a voice of great humility: 'Will you please buy the tea set which is displayed in that window? I want it for my wife. I have only roubles, and will repay you, with interest.'

I was delighted to be able to help him, and entered the shop, curious to see all their merchandise. I managed to secure the tea set, and paid in sterling. My Russian friend-in-need was waiting round a corner. I surreptitiously handed him the package. Tears of joy trickled down his cheeks. He insisted upon giving me extra roubles, and thanked me profusely.

I boarded the train for Murmansk later that day. We would have preferred to remain in the warmth of St Petersburg, but that was not permitted.

As we travelled north towards the Arctic regions, the landscape gradually changed. The scenery became flat and sharp; cold lakes, surrounded by fir trees, replaced the warm rounded country scenes near St. Petersburg.

After some hours, we halted at the wooden house which signifies the beginning of the Arctic Circle. Everyone rushed to photograph the uninspiring, yet symbolic, structure.

The temperature had dipped considerably, and I searched in my luggage for warmer clothing. St. Petersburg had been hot and sunny, but now there was an Arctic chill in the air.

I checked in at the hotel in Murmansk, and strolled round the city. The atmosphere was uncanny, for the sun was shining brilliantly, although it was late evening. The sun sets at midnight during this season.

It was a cold city - not merely because of the climate. I had a curious sensation. I felt that I was poised on the edge of the earth.

There was a strong odour of fish everywhere, and a wind which made walking unpleasant. A supermarket was open, but was poorly stocked. There was a large variety of tinned fish, but very little else. The discotheque sold brandy at £4 for a small glass. Well, I thought, in this city, I might be tempted to pay that amount for a glass of alcohol!

Life here is hard. During the deep winter months, from mid-December to the beginning of March, the sun never appears, and it is dark for 24 hours a day. The inhabitants compensate by using sunray lamps, and the streets are brilliantly lit. Children are given vitamins to supplement the deficiencies. Because of the snow-covered streets, the pavements are built high above the roads, to counteract the slush resulting from constant, heavy snowfalls.

At the spring equinox, there is a sun-welcoming ceremony, after the long period of darkness.

We visited a kindergarten school on the outskirts of the city. The children were obviously dressed for the occasion, wearing spotlessly clean dresses, with satin bows in their hair. The furniture was highly polished; portraits of Lenin peered down upon the children as they danced, and sang songs about him. We were invited to participate.

The headmistress, a plump, friendly, dark-haired woman, invited us, through an interpreter, to ask any questions about the Soviet system of education.

It was clear, from her replies, that communist ideology was implanted in the children's minds at an early age.

I made a comment: 'There seems to be an absence of religion in Russia'.

The headmistress replied: 'We are interested in living - and non-living!'

The school was open daily from 8am until 10pm, to enable parents to work. The teachers organized shifts. All education was free. Disabled and backward children were educated in a separate school.

After enjoying an excellent lunch at our hotel, we were driven to the docks, and shown over a huge refrigeration ship, which made frequent voyages to the Berent Sea, to collect thousands of tons of fish from trawlers, for storage in its gigantic hulls.

In the distance, a brilliant orange nuclear ice-breaker was at anchor, for use during the winter, to break the ice floes in the sea.

On the quayside, the tour leader was being interviewed by

a glamorous Russian broadcaster, attired in a smart, fur-trimmed, suede coat. A man in our party, who understood Russian, informed us that Carl was making critical comments on British politicians, in a broadcast to the Russian nation. The docks were even colder than the city, and I was glad to leave.

An enormous granite statue of 'The Unknown Soldier', many times larger than life-size, was situated on a bleak hill, overlooking the valley where thousands of Russian and German soldiers lost their lives when the Germans fought to within sixty kilometres of Murmansk, before being driven back, with heavy losses on both sides.

The authorities had planned yet another event. We arrived at a large building, known as 'The House of Friendship'. Such buildings existed in many cities in the Soviet Union, where discussions of all kinds took place.

Two officials in uniform showed us into a spacious room. We were seated at two long tables, and waiters hurried to serve us with tea and chocolate biscuits. Several Soviet officials then emerged, and sat at a long table, facing us.

Their interpreter announced: 'Now, you may ask any questions about communism, and the Soviet Union'.

Several of our companions stood up, and declared: 'I am a member of the communist party in Britain!'

With shining eyes, they conveyed greetings from their comrades in the North of England.

The event was beginning to take on an air of unreality for me, and I tried to convince myself that I was, in reality, face to face with communist party officials in this city at the top of Russia!

I was concerned about the future of young people born into such a challenging environment. I had seen a small group of teenagers in a park in the city. One of them was carrying an empty vodka bottle. 'What arrangements are made for the leisure hours of young people in this city?' I asked.

'We organize clubs for them. They are well taken care of,' said the official, through the interpreter.

Many other questions were asked, but there was always a slick reply, and it seemed as though answers had been prepared prior to the meeting.

Our visit to Murmansk was coming to an end. We departed the next morning, to return to St. Petersburg. When we were assembled on the train, the tour leader informed us that there would be a delay of two days in St Petersburg, due to problems on the Soviet railways. Our additional expenses would be borne by the Soviet Union.

It was good to be back in St. Petersburg, as it was pleasantly warm. I took a voyage across the Gulf of Finland to the Czar's Summer Palace, a beautiful relic of Old Russia. Fountains adorned the gardens. But there was torrential rain, so much of their beauty was lost.

I returned to the city, intending to visit the Hermitage, and was told that it took five years to view all the exhibits! The heat inside the building was intense, and I stayed only long enough to study the beauty of the architecture, and to hear a lecture, in English, on its history.

The staff of The Hermitage had struggled to maintain it throughout the last War, and had survived great hardship, sometimes surviving on berries.

The highlight of my second sojourn in St Petersburg was a visit to the opera. We were seated in boxes with a superb view of the show, and served with champagne and caviar. The opera appeared to portray the life of Mary, Queen of Scots. The priest wore a thick, black beard, reaching to his waist, which was far too long for a Scotsman!

On the last day of our stay, I discovered a Victorian hotel. The self-service restaurant was unlike any I had seen in the

West. Sumptuous dark red velvet armchairs surrounded the tables, and ornate, glittering chandeliers hung from the ceiling. The food was placed at one end of the huge room. Supplies were lavish, and diners could choose as much as they desired.

There was only one vacant seat, at a large circular oak table, occupied by about a dozen people. Bottles of vodka adorned the table, and it was evidently a special occasion, for they were toasting each other excitedly, and ignoring the dishes of delectable food on the table in front of them. They repeatedly tried to refill my glass, too, and proposed a toast to me!

Suddenly, they all rose, bade me farewell in Russian, and left me sitting alone at the huge table, surrounded by dishes of food, and empty vodka bottles!

Whilst I was in a queue for water in the street, I got into conversation with a man, who told me that he was a teacher of physical education. He had been allocated an apartment by the authorities, which was not to his taste, in an area of the city which he disliked. But he had no choice in the matter.

My last memory of Russia is of a plump woman, who assisted me on to the train, with my luggage, at St. Petersburg station. She smiled warmly at me, and I wished that I could have learnt more about her life, and her attitude to the regime at that time.

I was standing in the corridor of the train, enjoying a last glimpse of St. Petersburg, when I became aware of a Russian woman standing behind me. 'Are you travelling alone?' she asked me.

'Yes' I replied, 'I prefer to travel that way.'

'We never do anything alone,' she said, in a pious voice.

13. IDRIES SHAH

A visitor appeared at Coombe Springs in 1964.

I was sitting in my uncomfortable office, situated in a cold stone building near the main house. I was typing a book by Idries Shah, entitled *Special Problems in the Study of Sufi Ideas*. I was using what is now regarded as an antiquated method of printing, an electric typewriter. Computers were not yet in general use in offices. The right-hand margin had to be 'justified', giving the effect of a book.

I happened to glance out of the window, and noticed a man walking round the corner of the main house towards me. He was pushing a wheelbarrow, and wearing an all-in-one wartime camouflage suit. A cigarette dangled from the corner of his mouth. He wore a camouflage cap, pulled over his eyes. His apparent attitude and clothing shocked me. We had always been instructed by the Leader that, whilst performing our daily tasks, we should practise inner exercises, for example: 'remembering ourselves', sensing a limb, or other form of inner discipline.

It was quite apparent that this stranger was ignorant of these practices.

It was only much latter that I realized the significance of his appearance, and understood what he was endeavouring to accomplish: it was the destruction of an image, which we had clung to for many years. Now there was a possibility of gaining greater understanding of ourselves and our purpose.

I was typing the very book in which many of our present problems were explained. As I afterwards discovered, this book was written by the very man whom I have described.

I first met Idries Shah when he was invited by John

Bennett to meet the residents of the community. He came into the room, and Bennett pulled up an elegant armchair for him. To my astonishment, Shah instantly sat on the floor, cross-legged, and remained in that position for the duration of the meeting

One day, when I was working in the office at Coombe Springs, Idries Shah looked through the window at me, and pushed through a large folded document. 'Could you please have this document enlarged?' he said.

I took the document down to the printers, and got it enlarged, as requested.

A few days later, Shah looked through the window, and asked whether the enlarged document was ready.

'Yes, Mr. Shah' I said, in the way in which I always addressed him at that time.

He took the document, and said: 'Follow me!'

I walked behind him to the Lodge, where he was staying with his family, and followed him into the Study which had belonged to John Bennett in the days when he had lived there. It was now transformed into an Afghan room, with beautiful hangings and decorations.

Shah unfolded the document, and held it up in front of me. It was huge, and very powerful, with a design of an elaborate key.

I looked at it for what seemed to be several minutes, and then said: 'Thank you, Mr. Shah', and left the room, unable to express in words the experience which I had had at the sight of this extraordinary diagram. I think it was referred to later as 'The Key Diagram'.

I walked out of the Study, without any comment. It represented another language, which could not be expressed in words.

In 1970 Idries Shah offered me a job in the office at Langton Green. I was sitting at my desk one day when a

Helena in Langton days

stranger walked in. This was not unusual in those days, as many visitors came, hoping to have a talk with Shah.

'I want to see Idries Shah' he said, in an uncompromising tone. 'I have parked my caravan on the Green, and will not remove it until I have been granted an interview with him.'

'Just a minute' I said. 'I will go and ask him if he is free to see you. Wait here.'

I walked over to the main house, into Shah's study. 'There is a visitor who wants to see you, he has parked his caravan on the Green. He says he will not go away until you give him an interview.'

'Tell him', said Shah, 'that that is not the way to approach me!'

So I duly returned to the man, delivering Shah's message. He walked away without a word, drove his caravan off the Green, and was never seen again.

When I first came to work in the office at Langton, I took the opportunity to ask Shah a few questions which I thought at the time were important. But, as time passed, I realized that I did not appear to ask the right questions, for he usually changed the subject and spoke about something quite different. He often ended the interview with the remark: 'I need your co-operation'.

Upon reflection, I now think that I did not understand what he really meant, and consequently failed to act in the way he required.

I sometimes saw clearly that my request for his time was merely a call for attention - which, perhaps, I did not need anyway.

When I took my holidays, I usually decided to travel to a different culture, and as I had many friends, there were plenty of opportunities to do so.

On two occasions, when I returned to the cottage at Langton, where I lived, Shah came over from his family house on the estate, to greet me.

On these occasions, I was usually full of energy and excitement resulting from the many experiences I had had on my journeys.

When I answered his greeting with jubilation, he replied in a calm, quiet and unemotional voice: 'Everything here is exactly the same.'

When I reflected upon his tone of voice, it seemed that he was emphasizing the vast area between my experiences, and another realm where excitement and emotion were to be treated with reserve.

One evening at supper, Idries Shah got up and put his hand on the latch of the door, preparatory to leaving the supper room. I was sitting in front of him. He turned round and pointed to a glass on the table.

'There are two ways of looking at things. There is the usual way that we look at them, and there is also the way of looking at them as though each object is a veridical truth.'

A lady who was visiting Langton for the first time, came to supper one Saturday night when Shah was talking. She was trying to remember everything that he said. At one moment, Shah leaned forward towards her, and said to her: 'You do not need to remember everything I say!'

One of the students recounted to me that she was present at a conversation between Shah and a number of other pupils. 'Someone asked: "How can I practise self-observation?"

Shah answered: "You cannot practice self-observation at the time of the incident. You can, for instance, look back at the event later in the day, and see how, if you had behaved differently, things could have taken a different course."'

Speaking to an artist, Shah said: 'Paint your picture perfectly. Then, you will have time for this Work.'

On another occasion Shah was again asked a question about self-observation. He replied: 'You cannot do it at the time. What you could do is, at the end of the day, look back over the day, and see what you have done, how the day has gone. Do not flagellate yourself - we do far too much of that. But if you can, see the point at which you went off course, and look at it, and see how it could have gone differently.

It is like trying to steer a ship between icebergs.'

EPILOGUE

I retired in December 1989. Retired? It was 4am. A dense fog obscured the view across the Green.

A French friend had suggested that I might like to spend a few months in Paris, teaching English conversation to some of his friends who wished to improve their knowledge of English. Recently, I had participated in a crash course in English conversation for foreign students at Canterbury University, earning a diploma which would enable me to work abroad.

I was fortunate: a French family, who were going away on an extended holiday, had offered me their apartment in Paris for a few months..

I followed the road to Paris, sheltering behind a huge lorry taking the same route. I arrived in Paris at midday, and quickly found the address of the vacant apartment. The family were waiting there to welcome me.

It was impossible to park anywhere in the city. I had to travel by Metro to the homes of my pupils. This was easy, for the map of the Metro was easy to comprehend, and travel was cheap. I met a number of interesting people, including a woman who ran a publishing house - which was a formidable task for a female in Paris.

The experience that I gained in this way was invaluable to me, and when I returned to England, I eventually settled in Bath for some months. There, I was employed by an agency to teach English conversation to young students.

One evening, my doorbell rang, and when I opened the door, I saw a charming woman standing there. She said that she had heard a CD which I had made of some of my journeys. And asked whether she could come on my next trip to Morocco. As it happened, I was planning such a journey very soon. It was the first of a number of journeys which Karole Webster and I made together to Morocco, and enjoyed very much.

My next venture took me to London, where I participated in an eighteen-month course in Massage Therapy, run by Clare Maxwell-Hudson. Karole had previously completed this course several years before.

I moved to Tonbridge, and, a the end of the course, contacted Age Concern, which ran a centre in that town. At the rear of their premises, there was a large room, with all necessities for massage work, and I volunteered to run a clinic there once a week. It was very popular, and elderly people enjoyed the experience of massage - which many of them had never previously known

And then...